1c each

.... Box **$3.20**

chocolate "coins" covered
est, gilt bronze decorated.

"WILBUR" NUT LUNCH BARS

Suggested 10 for 10c Retailer

1769—240 in carton.

Carton $1.85

oz., sweet milk choco-
e, filled with roasted pea-
ts, double wrapped.

TOOTSIE ROLLS

Y-1210—100 rolls
ton.   **Carton**
23 sugar wafers
asstd. colors and
Largest penny roll on the
market!

RAINBOW "SWEETIES"

Y-1211—100 tubes in car-
ton.

Carton 67c

2 ¾ in. tube, filled with
candy pellets, asstd. colors
and f l a v o r s, transparent
face opening.

"BABY RUTH" MINTS

Y-343—Chocolate
Y-344—Mint
Y-345—Wintergreen
Y-346—Orange **Box 72c**
          100 rolls in box

"BABY RUTH" FRUIT DROPS

Y-327—Lemon
Y-328—Lime

Y-337—100 in box.
          Box
"Ostrich Egg" — Soft
white marshmallow
chocolate coated, w

Y-330—100 in box.
          Boz
"Butter Finger"—Ov
oz., peanut butter
chocolate coated, wra

Y-334—100 in box
          Box
"Buy Jiminy"—Over
peanut bar, wrapped

Y-335—100 in box
          Box
"Milk Nut Loaf"—
creamy marshmallow
ter, roasted nut mea
ping, allover coated
heavy milk chocolate

COMMONWEALTH OF PENNSYLVANIA
OFFICE OF THE GOVERNOR
HARRISBURG

THE GOVERNOR

GREETINGS:

It gives me great pleasure to congratulate the Pennsylvania Manufacturing Confectioners' Association (PMCA) on its 100th anniversary.

For decades, Pennsylvania's fresh dairy resources, transportation infrastructure, and quality workforce have enticed and retained candy manufacturers, which have become a major sector of our economy and a proud part of our heritage. I am greatly encouraged by PMCA's outstanding efforts to represent the interests of confectionery manufacturers, cultivate new business leaders, and create a network of support for promising endeavors. It is my hope that, with your continued assistance and advocacy, we can work together to set a bold course for the future and ensure that the confectionery industry remains a vital part of our commonwealth.

As Governor and on behalf of all Pennsylvanians, I congratulate everyone involved with PMCA on achieving this impressive milestone. Best wishes for a terrific celebration as well as unprecedented prosperity and growth in the next 100 years.

Edward G. Rendell

EDWARD G. RENDELL
Governor
June 2007

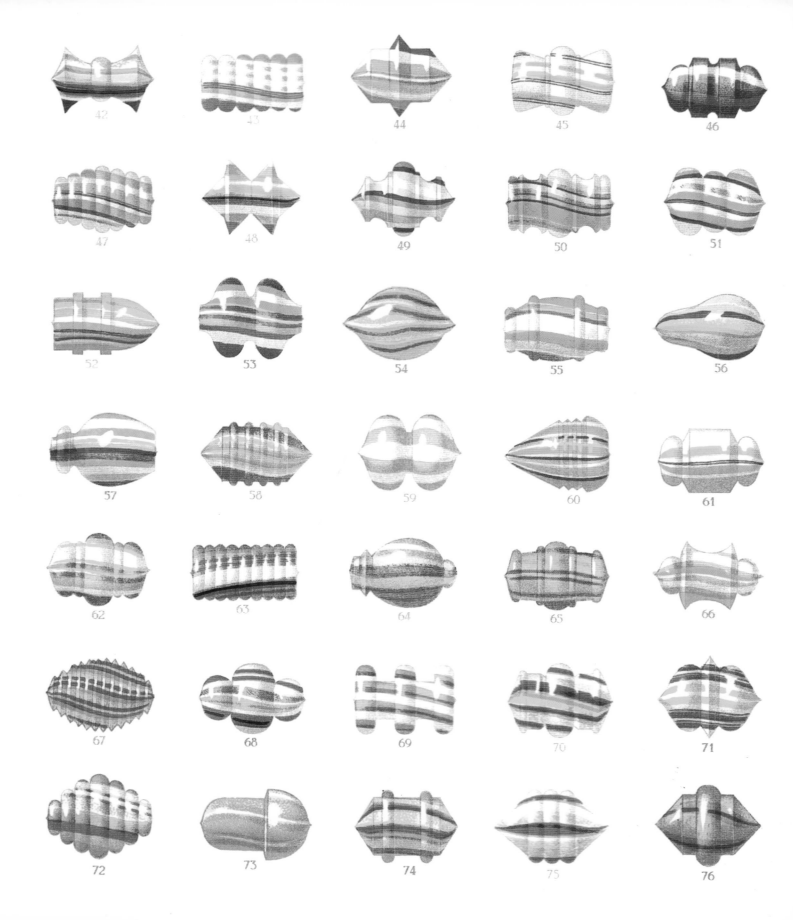

SWEET TIMES

100 Years of Making Confections Better

A **PMCA** RETROSPECTIVE

Beth Kimmerle

Project Managers: Yvette Thomas, Melissa Scheib, Eric Schmoyer, Reg Ohlson,
Rodney Snyder, Adrian Timms and Mike Allured
Designer: Randall Heath

Library of Congress Cataloging-in-Publication Data
Kimmerle, Beth 1969-

Sweet Times: 100 Years of Making Confections Better, A PMCA Retrospective /
Beth Kimmerle.—1st American Edition, 128 pages

ISBN 978-1-933430-19-5 (hardcover)
Library of Congress Control Number: 2007932873

1.Confectionery--History 2.Chocolate 3.Candy

Printed in South Korea by:
Star Print Brokers
Bellevue, Washington
www.StarPrintBrokers.com

This book is available at special discounts for bulk purchases, premiums,
and promotions. Special editions, including personalized inserts or covers,
and corporate logos, can be produced in quantity for special purposes. For
further information contact: PMCA, 2980 Linden Street, Suite E3, Bethlehem,
PA 18017 Telephone: +1 610-625-4655

Previous Page: Colorful candies or "bon bon" shapes and styles available in a
vintage German confectionery machinery catalog titled, *Bonbonmaschinen*. This
illustrated plate is from the 1866 catalog, which is housed in the PMCA library.
Image: PMCA archives

Table of Contents

Wouldn't *you* like some candy?

If you were a "solid sender" and you were having your first date with a gorgeous "dream boat" who could really cut a rug and you wanted to start "cookin' with gas," how's about saying, "Wouldn't *you* like some *candy?*"

If you were a convalescent and you'd dutifully eaten everything you were supposed to eat but none of it seemed to taste as good as usual, wouldn't *you* like some candy?

If you were a fisherman and that big one you'd been playing for 20 minutes had just slipped off the hook and you were feeling disappointed and tired and hungry, wouldn't *you* like some candy?

If you were a watch repairman and you'd been peering into dozens of watch cases and midafternoon found you craving something delicious and pep-restoring, wouldn't *you* like some candy?

Sure... Most everybody likes Candy!

IN BOX

IN BAR

IN BAG

CANDY IS DELICIOUS FOOD

Enjoy some every day!

COUNCIL ON CANDY of the NATIONAL CONFECTIONERS' ASSOCIATION...One North La Salle Street, Chicago 2, Illinois

©1947-NCA   ...an organization devoted to the dissemination of authoritative information about candy

Wouldn't you like some candy?

If you were a baby sitter and time was starting to drag and you craved something that would pep you up and still be kind to your tummy, wouldn't you like some candy?

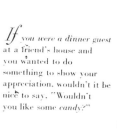

If you were the drummer in a dance band and those "hot breaks" you'd been beating out had you a little fagged and you knew that after intermission you'd be playing until 2 a. m., wouldn't you like some candy?

If you were a railway mail clerk and you'd been on your feet for hours sorting a mountain of mail on a streamliner and you felt the need of an energy "lift," wouldn't you like some candy?

If you were a dinner guest at a friend's house and you wanted to do something to show your appreciation, wouldn't it be nice to say, "Wouldn't you like some candy?"

Of course...Most everybody likes Candy!

IN BOX

IN BAR

IN BAG

CANDY IS DELICIOUS FOOD

Enjoy some every day!

COUNCIL ON CANDY of the NATIONAL CONFECTIONERS' ASSOCIATION...One North La Salle Street, Chicago 2, Illinois

© 1947—NCA   ...an organization devoted to the dissemination of authoritative information about candy

Vintage 1947 NCA candy advertisements promoting candy. Sure...most everyone does like it!
Credit: Beth Kimmerle Collection

Author's Note

I was in the back room of a candy company sifting through dusty boxes filled with newspaper clippings, quarterly catalogs and small black and white pictures when the company owner jokingly asked, "What is so interesting about all this old junk?"

But he and I both knew why I was there.

PMCA has played a vital role in candy history and I have been pleased to play a part in its 100-year anniversary project. I valued the opportunity to further explore my own interest in confectionery history and to look deeper into the last hundred years. I also liked the task of looking at a specific region of American candy makers and attempting to understand how and why they settled in Pennsylvania. This book was pieced together from PMCA archives, imagery and interviews with folks and vital historical information from member companies that have been, and continue to be, essential to this organization.

He and I both knew that I was not simply working on the history of an industry or organization but rather exploring a family tree.

The family of confection is strong. PMCA is one hundred years old, has held over sixty production conferences and boasts hundreds of members. I could see why PMCA wanted a book documenting their history. Not only was the group celebrating a milestone, but also it has evolved from a simple regional organization to one that is international with a new focus. The main objective of taking the time and expense to produce this book is not only to enable us to appreciate our industry history but also to help us celebrate it. In keeping with the PMCA's educational mission, this book is also an aid to help each of us experience confection trends and insights in a new way and to take a look at what the past means to our business and to us personally.

The book offers a way for PMCA to leave a legacy in its own library. As we become an international organization and our confection industry focuses on new trends and technology, it is an opportune time to pay tribute to the people, companies and brands that helped us grow and to leave a record for future generations.

A sincere acknowledgement must be made to the contribution of the PMCA History Book sub-committee. Eric Schmoyer, Reg Ohlson, Rodney Snyder and Adrian Timms brought wisdom, expertise and amusement to this project. Developing a book of this nature while working within this group allowed for insights and efficiencies that were incredibly valuable to the project.

Melissa Scheib and Yvette Thomas, also part of the PMCA History Book sub-committee, played special roles in making this book coalesce with speed and dignity. As part of the PMCA home office team they caught and released details, emails, photos and information at lightning speed and were essential spirited partners in making the many details unite into a book.

Our group asked Mike Allured, Ron Bixler and Rick Russell for special favors of reading and writing. They complied and their valuable contributions make this book richer as a result.

I am honored to have worked with the countless folks who contributed to this project, those mentioned and the many others who supplied material, encouragement and interviews. This support role is what PMCA is all about. It's an organization made up of members who are working together towards a common goal to enrich our entire confectionery industry.

This project was enjoyable to research but was not without its challenges. To make the project work we had to be both sentimental and scientific as well as patient and persistent. Collecting material and cultivating it into something readable, interesting and enduring is a proud goal. I thoroughly enjoyed the process of bringing this book to print and wish that you, the reader, will enjoy the results.

Candy and chocolate companies create fond memories and good times for their consumers but now it's your turn to enjoy a trip down memory lane. This book is dedicated to all PMCA members past and present and to honor their years of participation and experience. Without you, there is no history.

—Beth Kimmerle, Author
Sweet Times: 100 Years of Making Confections Better, A PMCA Retrospective

Foreword

Perhaps I was not conscious of it at the time, but I already knew the answer to the childhood question of "what do you want to do when you grow up?" At least, "something to do with confectionery" would probably have rated very highly. Candy is something we all learn to love from an early age, and we carry that fondness through our adulthood. Confections are designed to bring moments of delight to anyone, at any place, and at any time. It may be a reward for working extra hard, a consolation when jilted or feeling glum, a gift that says "I think you are special," something to share with friends, a moment to escape life's pressures, or one of countless other ways to make us feel better. Small wonder, then, that I should find it so much fun to work in the confectionery industry!

On reflection, though, I realize that is not the only reason. There is something about this industry, something so compelling, that many of us can think of nothing better than being intimately involved with the conception, design, manufacture, selling and consumption of confections.

Once active in the industry, few of us ever care to leave it. A good part of it lies in the nature of interaction of the folks who represent the companies that make up the confectionery industry. Don't get me wrong. Rival candy companies are fiercely competitive with each other, and the battle is intensely fought for space on the shelf, and for share in the hearts of consumer. Just as with rival sports teams, though, the combatants are bound by a common respect and love for the game. They also recognize that collaboration "for the good of the game" makes the industry stronger and, with that strength, provides continuing opportunity for their own companies.

It was just so for a group of entrepreneurial chocolate and candy makers one hundred years ago. One can picture a cigar smoke-filled room in a hotel in Philadelphia, where owners and representatives of these companies got together to form an industry association. They chartered the Pennsylvania Manufacturing Confectioners Association (PMCA) in 1907, in the court of Philadelphia. The aim was to form an organization through which they could work together to address common issues, and to set in place an environment for the manufacture and marketing of confections, so that the industry would grow to the benefit of all: manufacturers, suppliers, retailers and consumers. It was not the *only* trade association for confectioners, but over the decades has grown to be one of the most important, especially in regard to technical and manufacturing resources. PMCA has a significant role in the confectionery industry not just in Pennsylvania, nor just nationally, but internationally. In many respects, the emergence of the famous household names that comprise the companies of PMCA, the growth of the confectionery industry and the evolution of PMCA are interwoven strands of a fascinating fabric.

As current president of PMCA, I have the privilege of serving at a time when the association gets to celebrate the centennial of its existence. At the same time, we are at a bridge to an exciting future. As we chart our course for the next century, I can only hope that I, and the leaders who will follow me, will serve the industry, its retailers and consumers, as well as those who have brought us this far. Much has happened in ten short decades, and many volunteers have dedicated themselves to making confections better for us all.

PMCA has always been a volunteer organization, with only the office of secretary drawing remuneration. After four years of relatively informal activity, it was in 1911 that the association developed an executive structure, a constitution and by-laws. At that time, the stated object of PMCA was "to advance the standard of confectionery in all practicable ways." This holds true today, although stated somewhat differently in the mission and vision statements. The first annual convention was held in 1912.

From the early days, PMCA cooperated with other trade associations, particularly the National Confectioners Association, in order to serve its members. In the four decades leading up to the Second World War, much of the attention was on commerce and fair trade, although pooling of resources was evident as early as 1912, when analytical chemistry services, as well as collective shopping for insurance, were arranged for common access by members. The legislative agenda dealt with issues of compliance with the National Food Act of 1906, child labor, women's employment, employer liability and workmen's compensation. Unfair taxation on candy as a luxury was fought, winning the eventual repeal of the excise tax. Ethical code of conduct and the standardization of trade practices were strong. As the First World War gave way to the Roaring Twenties, attention turned to the role of "jobbers"—wholesalers supplying the retailers—and how they could best profit the entire industry. The industry faced many economic issues during the depression years of the 1930s, placing more emphasis on the self-policing of trade practices and the code of standards for members to follow. The activities at that time reflect coming to terms with the New Deal and how it could help the whole industry.

Many leaders of the industry served their country in various capacities throughout the wars of this century. It was after the Second World War that

PMCA began to deal increasingly with the technical and operations interests of its members. A sanitation committee helped members improve the cleanliness and quality of their operations. In 1947, PMCA gave birth to twins: the Annual Production Conference and the Research Program. These initially interconnected activities, nurtured through the leadership of Hans Dresel and Rudolph Kroekel respectively, started at Lehigh University. The programs later moved to Franklin & Marshall College in Lancaster, Pa., and later assumed more independent existence. The Production Conference found a home in Hershey, Pa. With the later addition of the short course education and training program, these three activities became the "core planks" that differentiate and constitute the essence of the mission of PMCA today. Much of what is said about how to make candy is said authoritatively in papers at the Production Conference. The research program, through sponsoring research at universities, has added to the wealth of technical know-how that helps confectioners make better products. In the late 1940s, research was trying to determine the nature of fat bloom defects in chocolate; now we have mathematical models with which to guard against such quality issues. The short courses are valuable technical training for participants from several countries.

In the latter part of the 20th century, PMCA increasingly was serving members beyond the Commonwealth of Pennsylvania. In spite of worldwide industry consolidation, PMCA today numbers around 400 member companies, based in various parts of the globe, but many that retain a strong manufacturing interest in Pennsylvania. Throughout this rich history, the confectionery industry has grown up to be a responsible adult. It exhibits fair trade practices, sound technical stewardship and enables the shopper to have the confidence and trust that the product that they buy will be honest, safe and of good quality. Industry associations such as PMCA deserve some credit for this. As we get ready to launch into the next century of exciting growth, I invite you now to turn the pages and celebrate 100 years of making confections better. Have fun, and enjoy!

—Adrian Timms, The Hershey Company
PMCA President
May 2007

The Hershey Kiss commemorates its 100th anniversary along with PMCA. Hershey's Kisses Chocolates were first introduced on July 7, 1907, at a time when each chocolate piece was wrapped in foil by hand.
Image Courtesy Hershey Archives

PMCA TIMELINE

1907

A group of Pennsylvania confectioners come together to improve and preserve the integrity of the confectionery industry. This group was chartered on January 26, 1907 in the Court of Philadelphia County, as the Pennsylvania Manufacturing Confectioner's Association. Today this group is known as the PMCA, An International Association of Confectioners. Founding companies include: Oxford Confectionery, Hershey Chocolate, and D.L. Clark Company.

1912

Whitman's introduces their first Whitman's Sampler box.

1915

The first Pennsylvania Farm Show opens as a place to proudly display Pennsylvania produced products. Today, the show is a weeklong event showcasing regionally manufactured goods, products and agriculture. The PMCA booth remains a show favorite.

1921

The Manufacturing Confectioner prints their first journal regarding the candy, chocolate and confectionery industry.

1911

Gaining membership from the original 7 companies, a total of 24 companies held a reorganization meeting of PMCA and began to officially record and document their meetings and events.

1912

Companies attending the annual meeting include: Wm. H. Luden and Quaker City Chocolate and Confectionery.

1920

Howard B. Stark originated the first caramel and swirled nougat pop known as a Snirkle.

SNIRKLES
The really GOOD 5¢
CARAMEL BAR
By The Makers of STARK

1921

J.N. Collins first produces Walnettos. It quickly becomes a popular nut filled caramel penny candy. Later in 1929, Collins Candy Company is bought by Peter Paul Candies.

1927

Philadelphia's Blumenthal Chocolate Company first produces Raisinets. The chocolate covered raisins join brands Sno-Caps and Goobers as movie time favorites.

1922

Goldenberg's Peanut Chews are first made in Philadelphia and they soon become popular along the East Coast. Three generations of the Goldenberg family later serve as PMCA presidents.

1925

Candy maker Henry Heide makes fruit flavored Jujyfruit to join his already popular Jujubes. Peter Van B. Heide is president of PMCA in 1981.

1930

D.L. Clark introduces his Zagnut candy bar.

OO Years 1907-2007

1924

Frank C. Mars introduces a new nougat bar to the universe. His Mars Milky Way Bar hits the galaxy.

1926

Paul Beich introduces the Whiz Bar. The slogan "Whiz—best candy bar there iz-z!" helps the candy bar remain popular for years.

1923

PMCA member companies are encouraged to use the slogan "Remember, Everybody likes Candy" on their stationeries and letterhead.

1928

Reese's Peanut Butter Cups make their debut. Farmer and former Hershey employee, H.B. Reese, concocts them.

1935

Gretchen Schoenleber, president of Ambrosia Chocolate Company, is the first woman to join a commodity exchange, The New York Cocoa Exchange.

1932

Just Born moves from Brooklyn to Bethlehem, PA and begins producing confections in the former Croft & Allen Candy factory.

1942-45

Women working on the Whitman's Sampler production line slip encouraging notes to soldiers in candy boxes destined for overseas shipment. The secret notes resulted in several long-term friendships and a few marriages.

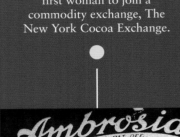

1939

Boyer Candy Company moves to a bigger plant in Altoona, PA to produce their Mallo Cup.

1940

Just Born introduces their panned candy favorite Mike and Ikes

PMCA TIMELINE

1934

During the Depression era, the president of the PMCA is authorized to appoint a Legislative committee to investigate proposed legislation that may affect the candy industry and its prospects for a quick and strong fiscal recovery.

1941

M&M'S are introduced. They are easy to eat, heat resistant and become popular wartime favorites for soliders.

1936

The 5th Avenue Bar, today produced by Hershey, is launched by Luden's.

1944

PMCA membership is opened to western area Pennsylvania companies and a Golf Committee is established to formally organize what's been a PMCA activity since its early years.

1947

The premier PMCA Production Conference is held at Lehigh University where it will remain for 6 years. The PMCA Nominating Committee and the Research Committee are established. Research at Lehigh University under the directorship of Dr. H.A. Neville focuses on "fat bloom."

The Pennsylvania Manufacturing Confectioners' Association

Production Conference

Lehigh University   Bethlehem, Penna.

September 8, 9, 10, 1947

In cooperation with the Lehigh University Institute of Research

1954
Bill Duck begins his tenure as official PMCA food scientist and concentrates his initial research on chocolate bloom, graininess in hard candy and consistency in marshmallow, starch candy and caramel.

1963

R.M. Palmer expands its Easter line to include Christmas confections. Later, hearts would join the molded chocolates as Valentine's Day products are created.

1965

At PMCA's 19th Annual Production Conference held in Lancaster, PA there are 354 registrants. Over four hundred partygoers attended the dinner banquet.

OO Years 1907-2007

1949

Created by a young girl recovering from polio, Candy Land is released by the Milton Bradley Company. The first Candy Land board games retail for $1.00 each.

1962

Hans F. Dresel, confectionery research advocate and founder of PMCA's Production Conferences dies.

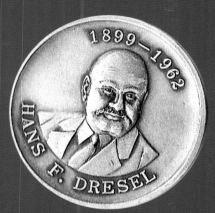

1899–1962

HANS F. DRESEL

1959

Candy companies sponsor national TV shows including: Tootsie Roll with Captain Kangaroo and Luden's with Rawhide

1963

A test program of the fat bloom inhibitor under Bill Duck's patent is studied to determine its effectiveness in coatings used under commercial operating conditions.

CANDY IS DELICIOUS FOOD
ENJOY SOME EVERY DAY!

1967

Giving new meaning to "Candy is Delicious Food", a new public relations committee is established to work closely with the National Confectioners Association in combating any advertising deemed detrimental to the industry.

1973

The first annual PMCA seminar for research sponsors is held. These seminars were held every January and the meeting was dedicated to the discussion of the new and immediate problems, products and processes affecting the chocolate and confectionery industries.

1976

Introduced by Herman Goelitz Candy Company, Jelly Belly Jelly Beans offer consumers unusual flavors in a tiny jelly bean.

1971

PMCA celebrates the 25th Annual Production Conference.

PMCA TIMELINE

Twenty Years of Confectionery and Chocolate Progress

From the Proceedings of the 1947 to 1966 Annual Production Conferences of the Pennsylvania Manufacturing Confectioners' Association

1971

The Candy Americana Museum opens at the Lititz, PA Wilbur Chocolate Factory. The historic chocolate site houses Penny Buzzard's chocolate memorabilia collection.

1974

Pennsylvania Dutch Candy buys famous mint maker Katherine Beecher Candies.

1970

"Twenty Years Of Confectionery and Chocolate Progress" from the proceedings of the 1947-1966 Annual Production Conferences is published by the PMCA.

Reese's Pieces Peanut Butter

1978

Reese's Pieces panned peanut butter bits are launched.

1980

Honoring a regional candy tradition, old-fashioned maple sugar hard candy drops made with Vermont maple sugar are one of the official confections sold at the Winter Olympics in Lake Placid.

1983

Nestle purchases Ward-Johnson Confections taking on classic brands like Oh Henry, Goobers and Sno-Caps.

Paul S. Dimick

1986

Walt Disney World celebrates "The Wonderful World of Chocolate" and selects Professor Paul S. Dimick of Pennsylvania State University, head of the PMCA's cocoa and chocolate research program, to be an authoritative speaker at their event.

OO Years 1907-2007

1981

M&M / MARS increases the size of its candy bars without increasing the price and therefore increases productivity without increasing inflation. This strategy opens new doors and increases the total confectionery market.

1985

PMCA's Research Committee publishes a book called "Abstracts of a Fondant Literature Search." It was available to members for the price of $25.

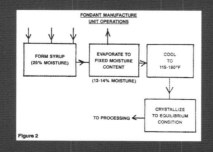

PMCA
An International Association of Confectioners

1986

The Board of Directors establishes an official PMCA logo.

1989

The PMCA Graduate Fellowship for Confectionery Research at The Pennsylvania State University is established through an endowment to honor the memory of outstanding past leaders of PMCA. Part of the PMCA mission is a commitment to foster the education and training of future technical and manufacturing leaders in the confectionery industry.

PMCA TIMELINE

1990
PMCA starts the Short Course Program and offers a class on caramel making. The class is held at Classic Caramel Company in York, Pa.

1996
PMCA Lifetime Service Awards are presented to Mr. Silvio Crespo, Mr. Walter Kalbach, Jr., Mr. Robert F. Keppel, Jr., Mr. William Medlicott, Mr. Duane Poulterer, and Mr. A.C. (Herk) Pulakos

1999
The premier PMCA Back to Basics program is held at the Annual Production Conference. The topic is "Nut Meat Ideas and Applications."

2003
PMCA gets a long-awaited permanent home. The PMCA office officially opens in Bethlehem, Pennsylvania.

1993
Boxed chocolate company, Russell Stover, pays $13.5 million for Whitman's Chocolate.

2000
Volume 1: The First 48 Years of Production Conference Proceedings is published and available on CD-ROM.

2001
PMCA's website is updated for easy navigation with useful features.

1997
The first PMCA Marie Kelso Memorial Award is presented to Edward Seguine of the Guittard Chocolate Company. It is awarded each year to the author of the paper presented at the previous year's Annual Production Conference that most significantly contributes to industry knowledge.

2002
An important revision of the PMCA 1990 by-laws is made, in which active or voting membership is extended to candy manufacturers outside the Commonwealth of Pennsylvania.

PENNSYLVANIA
MANUFACTURING CONFECTIONERS'
ASSOCIATION

FIRST
48
YEARS

Annual Production Conference
Proceedings
1947–1994

© Copyright 1996, Pennsylvania Manufacturing Confectioners' Association

2004

PMCA receives a letter of thanks from the Berlin Airlift Historical Society for garnering confectionery donations for the 100th Anniversary of the first flight by the Wright Brothers. The candy was parachuted over the Wright Brothers memorial as a commemoration of Col. the "Candy Bomber" Haverson's candy drop during the 1948-1949 Berlin Airlift.

2004
PMCA and the National Confectioners Association hold a joint short course in confectionery technology entitled "Chewing & Bubble Gum Confections Workshop" at the University of Wisconsin, Madison. It is a great success and the two associations begin a trend holding one joint course per year.

2006

The PMCA's Supplier Exhibition, held during the Annual Production Conference, is sold out for the first time since moving to the larger, Great American Hall at the Hershey Lodge and Convention Center.

2007
PMCA celebrates its 100th Anniversary.

100 Years 1907-2007

2003
PMCA's Honorary Lifetime Director, Silvio Crespo, with his wife Edith Crespo, provide a $50,000 endowment to the Pennsylvania State University Food Sciences Department.

2005
The PMCA website gets revamped with on-line registration forms, keyword searching and ordering of conference proceedings as well as, member access to the list of research library books and documents.

2006
PMCA hosts its first joint course with CMA Australasia in Melbourne, Australia on the topics of "Sugar Free Confectionery" and "Nutritious Confectionery and Snacks." Course leader, representing PMCA, was past PMCA Education and Training Chair, Maurice Jeffery of Jeffery Associates.

2007
PMCA publishes the first Back to Basics training series book. It's a compilation of *Back to Basics* seminars from 1999 through 2006. The Back to Basics programs are one of the most popular educational and training resources in confectionery technology.

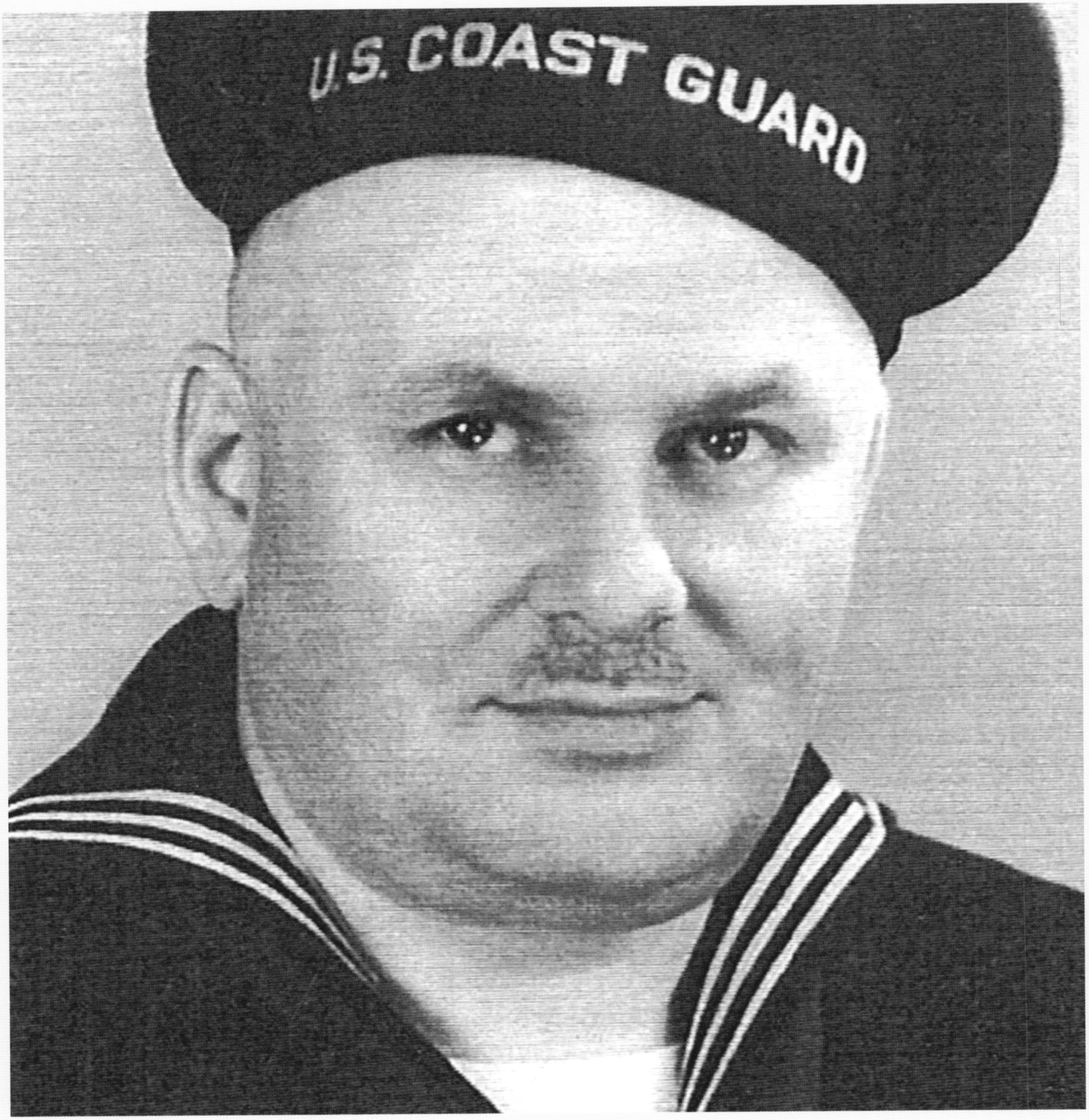
U.S. COAST GUARD

Chapter 1

Hans F. Dresel

Hans Dresel was raised in Germany and came to the United States in 1924 as a young man. Hans attempted to enter the U.S. Army during WWII, but his thick German accent and German military background set him back. Undeterred, he instead served locally in the US Coast Guard auxiliary on the Delaware River during WWII.

By 1947, he was employed as a sales representative for Felton Chemical Company. He referred to himself as a "flavor peddler," but sales was not his primary passion. Bill Duck, one of the first researchers for PMCA remembered Hans in 1986 in his Memorial Speaker speech, "I had been working in the laboratories of American Stores Company. Hans called on me as the representative for the Felton Chemical flavor house. When he called on me, he talked mainly about PMCA." Selling flavor took a backseat to PMCA. He was involved in the organization for almost twenty years.

As a member of the PMCA's Research Committee, Hans initiated the first Annual Production Conference. While on the committee, Hans started discussions regarding a "Production Symposium" that would last three days and take place at Lehigh University. PMCA members could send their foremen or company representatives to hear lectures and speakers discussing various candy topics.

Understanding that candy making in the 1940s was more of an art than a science and acknowledging that candy makers kept old-fashioned "secrets," Hans intended to bring industry folks together through sharing, learning and research. He convinced candy makers that they really had no mystery knowledge and that the answer to their common problems could be obtained through group study and discussion.

The premier working conference was held at Lehigh University in Bethlehem, Pennsylvania in September 1947 as planned, with a registration fee of $5 per day. The 65 attendees took candy courses on sugar and molasses, and learned about modern marvels such as air-conditioning and conveyors.

Hans Dresel served in the U.S. Coast Guard on the Delaware River during WWII.
Credit: PMCA Archives

After his successful initial program, Hans was appointed Chairman of the Organizing Committee of the Production Forum. The achievement of the first forum led to the subsequent annual conferences, held in the Spring of each year. For the second Conference in 1948, the registration fee was changed to $25 per person, which included two lunches on campus and a banquet. Attendance was limited to 200.

Hans was also responsible for the creation of the American Association of Candy Technologists. AACT originated from the first PMCA Production Conference where candy makers and technologists began to discuss the idea of organizing a national technical association. As part of this meeting, they discussed simple problems encountered in candy making, such as the boiling and inversion of sugar, why the candy was sticky, dull chocolate, and common problems that afflict candy making even today. The candy technologists met in 1948 and exchanged ideas to benefit candy technologists from across the United States. Early topics centered on sugar, corn syrup, starch and chocolate.

After WWII, Hans was instrumental in helping his native Germany rebuild a sweeter side. He often traveled abroad and encouraged German and European companies to interact with their American counterparts and share studies, research and technology. He laid important groundwork by encouraging European interaction at production conferences.

In his eulogy to Hans, Frank Poulterer, from Germantown Manufacturing and a longtime friend of Mr. Dresel's, mentioned that Hans also acted as a recruiter for Milton Hershey School.

Hans Dresel with wife Gertrude.

Dresel frequently asked members of the confectionery industry if they would hire potential candy makers trained at the Milton Hershey Vocational School. Forever involved in the education of future Production Conference attendees, he also proposed the popular course, "Candy Technology," at Drexel Institute in Philadelphia, Pa. By 1954, the Production Conference was moved to Franklin & Marshall College in Lancaster, Pa. and Hans continued his involvement in its coordination until his death in 1962.

In 1982, the PMCA decided to honor Hans Dresel's career by initiating the Hans F. Dresel Memorial Speaker designation at the Production Conference. The first speaker was from Cadbury Co. in England. Since then Memorial speakers have come from Germany, the Netherlands and the United States. The awardees are recognized for their long-term or ongoing technical contributions to the confectionery industry or for individual papers presented at the Conference.

During his distinguished career Dresel received numerous awards for his contributions to the confectionery industry, both in the US and also in his native Germany. Awards include; Knight's Cross Of The Order of Merit, IFT Merit Medal and an NCA Award of recognition.

In his honor there is also a Hans Dresel Memorial Scholarship fund. Scholarships are awarded to students interested in confectionery technology and majoring in food science at leading universities.

"There are those here tonight who may not know who Hans Dresel was. To forget this man would be a great loss to the industry. He was so unique and contributed so much, both as a member of the research committee and of the Production Conference. We need his story to help us know what is possible for the future. It is my hope that those who remember will begin to write down their memories of Hans so that we do not lose him."

—William Duck, First PMCA research director and Hans Dresel Memorial Speaker, 1986

A Hans Dresel commemorative coin was issued in 1971. It was given as a gift to all attendees of the PMCA Silver Anniversary Production Conference.

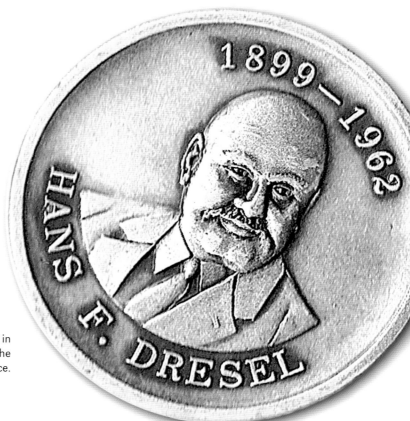

Chapter 2

Early Years: Founding Fathers and Philosophies (1907-1946)

PMCA BECOMES ESTABLISHED

In the same year that a first class postage stamp was worth two cents, Pennsylvania adopted its state flag and the first ball dropped in Times Square, a regional group of candy makers came together to cover production and other topics of the day. This group became chartered on January 26, 1907 as the Pennsylvania Manufacturing Confectioners Association. They formed their collaboration to increase strength with suppliers and to share thoughts about candy making recipes and production.

As manual labor was slowly replaced by confection machinery the number of confectionery manufacturers and wholesalers grew. This development of new equipment combined with easy transportation channels, inexpensive ingredients and a solid labor force had Pennsylvania confectioners expanding at an especially rapid pace. One of the biggest issues that surrounded candy makers at the turn of the century was food production safety and ethics. As candy makers were able to turn out more products, there was a growing concern about candy quality. Producing good candy was strongly linked to technique. An industry that was once comprised of smaller operations, mostly conducted out of home kitchens had grown up. As candy makers moved to large-scale factories, they faced new dilemmas with machinery, recipes, packaging and labor.

The early PMCA was a group of Pennsylvania confectioners who worked to improve and preserve the integrity of the confectionery industry and discuss general candy making issues. By 1911, the group had 24 members but with some hard work and appeal, the membership grew to 57 by the following year. The 1912 membership

A 1907 image shows a worker packing chocolate boxes at the Huyler's chocolate factory. White mobcaps were used as head covering for nurses and were a part of working women's garb into the early 20th century. Many chocolate companies, concerned with hygiene in their plants, adopted the headcovering that implied and instituted a clean and sterile working environment.
Credit: NYPL, Humanities and Social Sciences Library / Photography Collection, Miriam and Ira D. Wallach Division of Art, Prints and Photographs

number included local candy organizations: The Philadelphia Jobbing Association, The Pittsburgh Confectioner Club, Lackawanna County Jobbing Confectioners' Association and The Central Pennsylvania Jobbing Confectioners' Association. These regional groups banded together under the PMCA roof for candy connections and kinship, and to create a forum where those important confectionery topics of the day were discussed.

In its early years, members of the PMCA sought uniformity in food laws, purchasing power and, most importantly, camaraderie. But it seems like they also had some loftier goals. By 1912 they were interested in establishing a collective laboratory where "...analytical work could be done, for and on behalf of all members..."

This 1907 image shows women packing chocolate boxes. Although the Industrial Revolution had already taken place, women in the workplace was still a rarity. Early issues that PMCA members were concerned with were labor laws, product integrity and working conditions.
Credit: NYPL, Humanities and Social Sciences Library / Photography Collection, Miriam and Ira D. Wallach Division of Art, Prints and Photographs

In 1923

the Pennsylvania Confectioners' Association made an official declaration of a

CODE OF PRACTICE to govern all members of our Association

1. Whatsoever you would that men should do with you, do you even so unto them.

2. Avoid misrepresentation. Make an honest product and market it honestly.

3. In all advertising, the truth, the whole truth and nothing but the truth.

4. Set a high example to those with whom you deal, both in buying of raw material and the selling of finished product.

5. Be alert, kind and appreciative and you will thus be able to consistently expect the same from others.

6. Associate only with Houses and Representatives that do not practice deceit. Remember that nothing permanently profitable can come from double dealing.

7. Place the business of manufacturing candy on a higher plane. We believe that the candy business is a high class business. There is no honor in gain unless it results from clean methods, honest principles and a worthy product.

8. It is possible to co-operate with competitors with profit. Price cutting is a sign of weakness. Every successful institution should have for its ultimate aims a legitimate profit.

9. Be true to your country and its laws, your city, your fellow man and yourself— you can not then be untrue to your business or those from whom you buy or to those to whom you sell. By this standard too, you will be just to your competitors—and the esteem of your competitors is an asset not to be despised.

PHILLY CANDY WEEK

The Retail Confectioners Association of Philadelphia (RCAP) now hosts America's oldest show dedicated to the retail confectioner, The Philadelphia Candy Show. They were founded in 1918 for the purpose of sharing information and knowledge about candy making and retailing. The trade show is now called, "The Philadelphia National Candy Gift & Gourmet Show." Twice yearly it showcases various aspects of the candy making industry for gourmet retail confectioners, manufacturers and wholesalers.

This early Philadelphia Candy Show opened on February 5, 1910 and was reported on in the March 1910 issue of *Confectioners Journal*. The Philadelphia Confectioners' Association, The Philadelphia Jobbing Confectioners' Association and The Philadelphia Confectionery Salesmen's Association arranged the exhibition. The show featured entertainment including caramel wrapping, candy pulling and "cocoanut" opening. Among the exhibitors were: Croft & Allen Co., H.O. Wilbur & Sons, Inc., Thos. Mills & Bros., Hershey Chocolate Company, Brandle & Smith Co., Runkel Brothers Chocolate, Tootsie Roll and Henry Heide.
Image: Library Of Congress, Confectioners Journal

First Annual Convention of the Pennsylvania Manufacturing Confectioners' Association, Harrisburg, May 23 and 24, 1912

The first official convention of the Pennsylvania Manufacturing Confectioners' Association took place in Harrisburg, Pennsylvania in May of 1912. The *Confectioners Journal* reported on the PMCA meeting in their June issue of 1912. This group photo was taken, unfortunately without members names listed.

THE HOME OF **Hershey's** COCOA AND MILK CHOCOLATE

······· Section 2 ·······

PMCA: EARLY MEMBERS

The following companies are listed among the members at the first PMCA meetings. While early PMCA records are vague, these companies are listed on the roster for attending 1911 and 1912 annual meetings.

BACHMAN CHOCOLATE MFG.

In the early years, Bachman manufactured mostly chocolate coatings, but by the 1920s they were known for their bars, cocoa and nonpareils. In 1982, Wilbur Chocolate Co. acquired the Mt. Joy facility from Bachman Candy Co., which had been formerly owned by Peter Paul Cadbury. John Bachman served as PMCA president in 1932.

This early Hershey's printed cardboard display depicts the chocolate factory nestled in the Pennsylvania countryside. Fresh cow's milk and a train line for supplies and shipping are located nearby.

BLUMENTHAL BROTHERS

The Blumenthal Brothers Chocolate & Cocoa Company was started in 1911 in the Philadelphia area. First specializing in wholesale chocolate, the company manufactured their first candy product, nonpareils, in 1922. By the late 1920s, the company began marketing a mini version of traditional nonpareils under the trade name Sno-Caps. Their movie theater classics, Raisinets and Goobers, were added later and the brands were eventually sold to Nestle. Samuel Blumenthal served as PMCA president in 1963.

BRANDLE & SMITH CO.

By 1906, this Philadelphia-based candy maker had a block long factory on Ninth and Dauphin Streets. Primarily producing hard candy, they became famous for their signature oval ten-cent tins of Mello Mints and other "satin finish" candy specialties.

THE CASSIDY CANDY CO.

Mr. J. Clyde Cassidy graduated from the Altoona High School in 1912, and went on to attend Gettysburg College. After a brief stint in the lumber business with his father, he enlisted in the U.S. Army, 17th Machine Gun Battalion, Sixth Division. Following his discharge, he and his father formed a partnership and manufactured a variety of chocolate-covered candies.

D.L. CLARK

Irish immigrant and entrepreneur, D.L. Clark, originally entered the candy business as a traveling salesman with a horse drawn wagon. In 1886, Clark began to manufacture his own confectionery treats out of the backroom of a small house in Pittsburgh, Pa. His small company soon became a top tier candy manufacturer and his eponymous Clark Bar would soon emerge as one of the nation's best selling candy bars. By 1911, the company moved to a bigger production facility on Pittsburgh's North Side.

Clark shipped individually wrapped Clark Bars to American troops during World War I. The Clark Bar became extremely popular with the soldiers and its popularity carried over to the general public in the years following the war. By 1920, the D.L. Clark Company was making about 150 different types of candy, including several five-cent bars like Zagnut and Clark Coconut Crunch Bar.

With a booming candy trade, Clark began manufacturing chewing gum and soon the company was known for Clark's Teaberry and Tendermint gums brands. After ten years as a candy contender, Clark decided to specialize

HOME OF CLARK BAR

CLARK-BAR

Has a center of delicious creamy Caramel—highly spun jacket which is interwoven with fresh Peanut Butter and coated with a very special quality of Chocolate Coating, rich in Honest Chocolate flavor.

Its unusual eating quality and extra large size has made Clark Bar "First Choice" with millions of consumers.

Not much salesmanship is required to sell Clark Bar. Just a little effort and it will be your leading selling Candy Bar!

24 Count, 48 Boxes to the Case
Price per Box, $.65

The D. L. Clark Company
Pittsburgh, Pa.

exclusively in candy bars and sold their gum division. Teaberry gum is still made today.

In 1955, the Clark family sold their candy business to the Beatrice Food Company, which operated the company until 1983. The Clark Bar candy bar would have a few more owners including Leaf Inc. before settling in as a NECCO classic candy.

DE WITT P. HENRY CO.

Makers of No Kiddin!

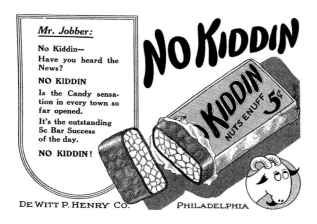

HARDIE BROTHERS

Started as an offshoot business of their father's biscuit company by the brothers Hardie in 1901, this company once devoted 5 acres of their factory to candy making.

HEIDELBERGER CONFECTIONERY

This self-coined "Philymade" Sweets company made boxed chocolates on N. Second Street in Philadelphia. Mark Heidelberger served as PMCA president in 1953.

HERSHEY

Upon selling his successful caramel business in 1900, Mr. Milton Hershey, built a chocolate manufacturing facility in Derry Church, PA. The town was soon renamed Hershey, PA and the factory would mass-produce 5-cent, milk chocolate bars. An early advertising slogan described this affordable new product as "a palatable confection and a most nourishing food."

Out of their bourgeoning factory, the Hershey Company soon produced Hershey's Kisses (1907), Mr. Goodbar (1925), Hershey's Syrup (1926), Krackel bar (1938), and Hershey's Miniatures (1939).

Milton S. Hershey died in 1945, at age 88, and the company maintains, "his deeds are his monument." Today, The Hershey Company is a foremost manufacturer of chocolate and non-chocolate confectionery and grocery products.

Confectioners Journal advertisement, he claimed to have sold 3 million packages of the drops in one season.

In 1927, Luden sold his outfit to Food Industries of Philadelphia but remained a confectioner involved in the trade throughout his life. By 1936, Luden's introduced the 5th Avenue candy bar and was making both cough drops and the popular 5th Avenue candy bars under contract to the government for military use during WWII. In 1986, Hershey Foods Corporation acquired Luden's and they continue to make the classic 5th Avenue candy bar today.

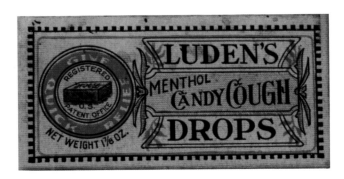

W. H. LUDEN

William H. Luden began his candy business in 1879 out of his mother's kitchen in Reading, Pa. and by 1910 owned a large production plant and produced an extensive confection assortment from cough drops to chocolates, marshmallow to mints. Luden's became best known for his 5-cent package of Menthol Cough Drops. In a 1906

OXFORD CONFECTIONERY

At the start of the 20th century, Oxford Confectionery Company of Oxford, Pa. produced sepia-toned collectible baseball cards with lithographed black and white images. The baseball player's name and team were printed at the bottom. A full set of Oxford's 1921 issue cards sell for over $6,000 today.

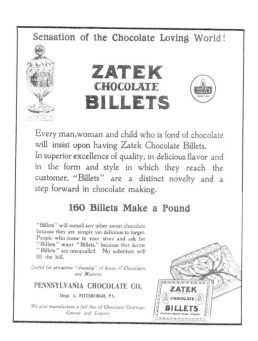

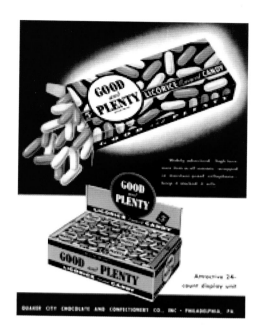

PENNSYLVANIA CHOCOLATE CO.

Started in 1906, this Pittsburgh, Pa. company produced a full line of coatings and cocoa along with popular candy products like Eatmors and Zatek Chocolate Billets.

PHILADELPHIA CARAMEL

Located in Camden, N.J., this company issued a legendary set of 25 color baseball cards in 1909.

QUAKER CITY CONFECTIONERY

The Quaker City Confectionery Company, founded by William B. Rosskam in Philadelphia, first produced Good & Plenty licorice panned candy in 1893. In 1950, with a catchy theme tune, Choo Choo Charlie, the cartoon train engineer who fueled his engine with Good & Plenty candy, first appeared in advertisements.

In 1973, Warner-Lambert purchased Good & Plenty candy and owned it until 1982 when the operation was purchased by Beatrice Foods and relocated the candy operation to St. Louis, Mo. In 1983, Huhtamaki Oy purchased Leaf Brands, the confectionery division of Beatrice Foods. Hershey Foods Corporation acquired the Leaf North America confectionery operations from Huhtamaki Oy of Helsinki, Finland in 1996.

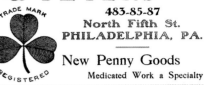

R.E. RODDA CANDY CO.

In a 1916 advertisement, The R.E. Rodda Candy Co. of Lancaster, Pa. tagged themselves, "The Jelly Bean House Of America." Not only did they make jellybeans, taffy and lollipops; they produced a seasonal line of marshmallow products. Its popular marshmallow Easter chicks were made by hand-squeezing marshmallow through pastry tubes to form a little yellow bird with wings. It was these items that inspired Bethlehem-based Just Born to purchase Rodda in 1953. Today, Just Born makes 1.2 billion Marshmallow Peeps every year for every holiday season.

SMITH & PETERS

Producers of Cough Tablets, Floral Dainties, Diadems and Cachous, this Philadelphia company was primarily a lozenge maker and was well known for their medicated candies and later candy cigarettes.

STANDARD CHOCOLATE COMPANY

This small chocolate company located in Cereal, Pa. made moulded chocolate pieces including "Twin Havana" cigars, wild animal and automobile shapes.

STANDARD CARAMEL CO.

Formally known as Lancaster Caramel, Standard Caramel Company made caramels and some penny candies. Started in 1886, Lancaster Caramel was founded by Milton S. Hershey. The caramel enterprise helped launch his Hershey Chocolate Company when he sold the company for $1 million in the year 1900.

With the growing popularity of trading cards and baseball, Standard Caramel got into the baseball card business. The 1910 issue Standard Caramel Honus Wagner baseball card is a favorite with card collectors and a card in good condition sells for about $2,500. The former Pittsburgh Pirate, Honus Wagner—also known as "The Flying Dutchman"—became the first baseball player to have his signature branded into a Louisville Slugger baseball bat in 1905.

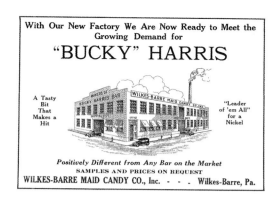

WILKES-BARRE MAID CANDY CO.

Producers of the "Bucky Harris" candy bar, this Wilkes-Barre, Pa. candy company honored the legendary sportsman with his own bar because he had achieved celebrity status in Pennsylvania. Harris learned to play baseball in the mining region of northeastern Pennsylvania and reached the major leagues in 1919. He was also an outstanding basketball player, playing professionally with local Pennsylvania teams during baseball's off-season. Harris went on to manage the Philadelphia Phillies in 1943 and led the Yankees to a World Championship in 1947.

WILLIAMSPORT CANDY MFG.

This company produced Peerless Brand Jelly Drops and Jelly Paste.

This 1906 print shows a group of children heading to the candy store to spend their pennies. In 1906 on the candy store shelves the children might discover Reed's Butterscotch hard candies, Quaker City's Good and Plenty or a stick of Y&S Licorice.

Credit: Beth Kimmerle Collection

PENNSYLVANIA'S CONFECTIONERY HISTORY: CHOCOLATE UNTIL THE COWS COME HOME

PENNSYLVANIA'S DAIRY INDUSTRY

In the 1600s, early immigrants to Pennsylvania brought cattle with them from Europe to supply their families and farms with both dairy products and meat. Although many different cattle breeds including Jersey, Guernsey and Brown Swiss were imported by early settlers, it was not until the late 1800s that cattle were bred exclusively for dairy purposes.

On early rural Pennsylvania farms, milk and dairy products were produced primarily for home or local use. However, with the movement of population from the farms to the cities at the turn of the 19th century, it became necessary to improve the production and distribution of milk. Significant inventions such as bottling, milking machines, pasteurization and refrigerated milk tank cars contributed towards making milk a commercially viable and healthy product.

As a result of its green pastures and hardworking and industrious farmers, by the end of the 1800s, dairy became Pennsylvania's foremost industry. To insure a steady supply, many food operations that depend on fresh dairy products moved into the state. Pennsylvania continued to have plenty of fresh milk and cream. To this day, dairy remains the largest part of Pennsylvania's agricultural industry and is the primary contributor to the entire state economy. Lancaster County alone is the top-ranking county in the nation for milk production.

With mammoth milk chocolate producers like Hershey, M&M Mars and Wilbur located in or near the Lancaster area, it may also be the top-producing region for milk chocolate.

A Pennsylvania State Seal from the 1850s.

43

FOOD PROCESSING IN THE KEYSTONE STATE

By the late 1800s, not only were cows plentiful in Pennsylvania, but chocolate and other food products were as well. By the turn of the century, Hershey was a major chocolate and cocoa wholesale supplier and manufacturer. Along with producing millions of 5-cent candy bars, Milton S. Hershey's prosperous company provided both large and small businesses with confection supplies necessary for candy making. Because all the vital ingredients needed for manufacture were nearby, many candy and chocolate companies saw Pennsylvania as an opportunistic place to open their factories and shops. As a result, food processing in general grew into a major Pennsylvania industry. Hershey's new Derry Township factory started turning out milk chocolate in 1905, the same year H. J. Heinz Company was incorporated. Both Milton S. Hershey and Henry J. Heinz are considered upstanding corporate leaders who were fair and loyal to their workers. Through their efforts, they led a movement for clean and bright factories based on the principle that workers deserve an agreeable work environment along with an opportunity for self-improvement and education. Watching their lead, many Pennsylvania food companies banded together and fight for federal legislation outlawing foods that had false labels and harmful chemical adulterations. This culminated in the passage of federal food legislation in 1906. The original Pure Food and Drug Act was passed by Congress on June 30 and signed by President Theodore Roosevelt regulating food, drugs and drinks.

In that same year, 1906, Italian immigrant Mario Peruzzi incorporated his business in Wilkes-Barre, Pa. His company, Planters Nut and Chocolate sells whole salted peanuts and produces peanut candy bars and chocolate-covered nuts. The Planters Company held a contest among high school students in the Wilkes-Barre area to design a character to help sell Planters product. In 1916 the loveable and spiffy Mr. Peanut was introduced to the world.

PLANTERS

All Progressive Confectioners should sell
PLANTERS PRODUCTS

Sold by all jobbers in
the metropolitan district

Planters Nut and Chocolate Co.

Wilkes Barre   Brooklyn, N. Y.   Suffolk
Foot of Joralemon St.
Phone Main 4422

This advertisement for Planter's is reprinted from a 1928 edition of The Confectioner. Mr. Peanut is said to be one of the most recognizable characters ever developed for a product.
Credit: Manufacturing Confectioner

By 1914, Pennsylvania passed a statewide food law stating that, "Mineral substances of all kinds, whether poisonous or not, are forbidden in confectionery." With the onset of prohibition and strong Mennonite wariness of alcohol they also concluded that the addition of any alcoholic liquor to confectionery would be prohibited along with any ingredient "...deleterious to health, or consists in whole of part of a diseased, contaminated, filthy or decomposed substance..."

PENNSYLVANIA RAILWAYS: LOCOMOTIVE AND LOCATION

Pennsylvania was a pioneer of early rail development and by 1860 there were 2,598 miles of rail track connecting Pittsburgh, Philadelphia, Reading and the Lehigh Valley. Throughout the century, Pennsylvania's rail systems continued to be developed and, by 1865, Pennsylvania trains are sending travelers and freight alike to New York, Washington, Buffalo, Chicago, and St. Louis. The Pennsylvania rail system became one of the great "trunk-line" railroads of the nation. Pennsylvania also developed a significant network of subsidiary lines within its own state borders. The Reading and Lehigh Valley systems expanded to become great carriers of freight and important links in the industrial economy of the entire Mid-Atlantic region. By the 1930s, all of the important train lines of the eastern United States passed through Pennsylvania. With rail passengers stopping off across Pennsylvania for rest, relaxation and food, towns on train lines benefited greatly from a train depot. Each town on every rail line

The Altoona, Pa. rail line was just one of the many important transportation arteries that Pennsylvania offered to confectionery businesses eager to deliver their freshly made goods and access a steady stream of cocoa and sugar supplies. This late 1800s stereoscopic photo was viewed through a special viewing device creating a three-dimensional image. A new way to see the world, stereoscopic images of travel pictures, landscapes and stories were sold by the millions.
Image: New York Public Library

stop boasts a fine candy store to allow travelers to shop for a box of assorted creams, lollipops for the children or a bag of horehound drops for the long trip. At its railroad best, Pennsylvania could claim more than 10,000 miles of railroad track with hundreds of stops and sweet shops in between.

Because Pennsylvania's rail line is so well connected, chocolate and candy companies could count on timely distribution of their fresh goods and rapid access to imported ingredients. Many confectionery companies were eager to open in the transportation hub of America. With a strong railroad system, confectionery makers essentially had a direct line to their consumers. Candy that was made in Philadelphia in the morning could be on a New York department store shelf by the next day.

PA PORTS AND WATERWAYS

Pennsylvania ports and waterways have always been of major importance for its commerce. The state has three major port cities: Philadelphia, Pittsburgh, and Erie, all of which are unique in location and offerings.

The Port of Philadelphia is the largest on the Eastern seaboard and includes four other cities along the Delaware River. Philadelphia is the largest freshwater port in the world and today boasts the second largest volume of international tonnage in the United States. While considered an inland port, Pittsburgh has always been a substantial center for shipping and receiving goods. Erie, Pa. situated on Lake Erie, is the central hub to the Midwest. It is the vital port of Philadelphia that has continued to supply a steady stream of imported sugar and cocoa beans needed to make chocolate and candy across the state.

In total, Pennsylvania's waterways have long provided ample outlets for its candy commerce and perishable goods: Eastern rivers link Philadelphia and other ports with the Atlantic Ocean; Western rivers link Pittsburgh to the Gulf of Mexico; and Lake Erie provides access to the St. Lawrence Seaway. Pa. has access to the Atlantic Ocean and the Great Lakes and connects with waterways and rivers such as the Delaware, Allegheny and Ohio. With its water byways, Pennsylvania was an early leader in water transportation and Philadelphia, Pittsburgh and Erie all developed as major port cities. All three have long been valued by confection and other businesses alike for their access to easy distribution.

A PLACE OF SUPPORT: GOVERNMENT INCENTIVES, HARDWORKING LABOR AND BOUNTIFUL LAND

With its rail lines directly connecting factories to customers and hard labor, many confectionery companies did not need much urging to move from other states like New York or New Jersey to bountiful Pennsylvania. In fact, in 1932, despite the Depression, Just Born moved their operation here from bustling Brooklyn, New York. The bourgeoning candy company opened a new factory in the former Croft & Allen plant in Bethlehem, Pa. and would become an important employer and community business in the recognized steel town. Just Born also received important incentives from Pennsylvania's government. Understanding commerce and with a desire to diversify, the government gave tax breaks and abatements to businesses that came from out of state. The Pennsylvania state government was keen on bringing good industry into the state both for its workers and long-term economy.

In this era, Pennsylvania's main labor force was comprised of many Mennonite and Pennsylvania Dutch (German) folks who were hardworking, devout and strictly anti-alcohol. Savvy chocolate companies intentionally set up shop in those regions where workers viewed drinking chocolate as a good and healthful alternative to alcoholic beverages. Furthermore, the Mennonites and the Amish brought distinction to the region through their "Pennsylvania Dutch" lifestyle, which to many business owners came to mean traditional,

moral and industrious laborers. This concept was not lost on Milton Hershey. Raised Mennonite himself, Hershey understood that his fellow Pennsylvanians would make a fine labor force and when looking for the ideal spot for his chocolate company, he ultimately broke ground just one mile from his childhood home.

The triple crown to setting up a confection business in Pennsylvania was the land. Not only pretty, it was also plentiful. In Pennsylvania there was enough for Mr. Hershey to ultimately purchase over 10,000 acres for his own chocolate operation and dairy farms and ample space for others to follow suit. With rolling hills and pastures, Pennsylvania was to confectioners both buildable and beautiful.

Pennsylvania is often referred to as the Keystone State, meaning it is a key part of a structure. The term "keystone" comes from architecture and refers to the central, wedge-shaped stone in an arch, which holds all the other stones in place and provides the central support. Pennsylvania's name is wholly justified when exploring the economic, social, and political development of confection companies. Pennsylvania has been a hub of sweet activity for many years.

This 1901 photo shows a typical Pennsylvania farm. Dairy remains one of the largest sectors of economy in Pennsylvania.
Credit: New York Public Library

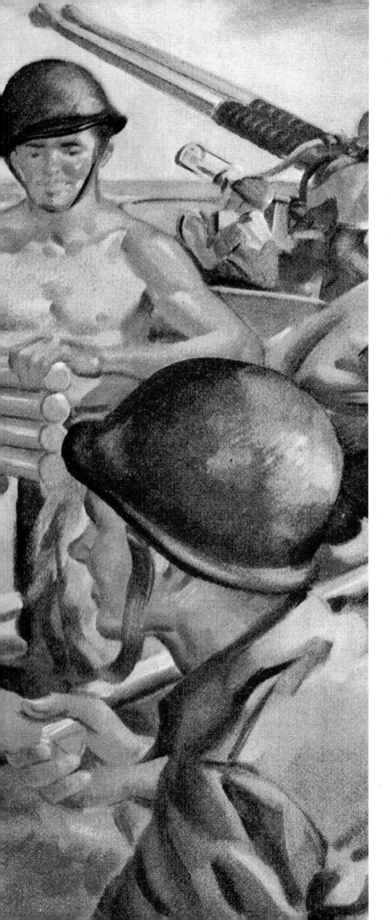

⋅ ⋅ ⋅ ⋅ ⋅ ⋅ ⋅ *Section 4* ⋅ ⋅ ⋅ ⋅ ⋅ ⋅ ⋅

AT HOME AND FAR AWAY: CANDY AT WAR

"The Sweets of commerce are making less horrible the bitterness of war. How desirable chocolate or candy may be, or what solace is obtainable from chewing gum, has been proven on the battlefield."

—*Confectioners Journal*, November 1918

Candy has a long history of wartime consumption and has been valued by soldiers as a source of energy for hundreds of years. In fact, Christian Crusaders, in their first trip to Syria in 1099, discovered Arabian sugar and named it "sweet salt" for its ability to deliciously preserve fruits and nuts. It became a necessary ingredient on their long journeys from home and soon became used as an exclusive and expensive spice and sweetener throughout Europe.

Even pre-Columbian soldiers consumed goblets of chocolate before battles. Both Mayan and Aztec priests offered cacao seeds to the gods and served chocolate drinks during sacred ceremonies. Aztec warriors used cacao to fortify themselves in battle.

Candy was advertised as giving quick energy to our fighting men. This WWII National Confectioners Association advertisement shows Navy men taking a break to share a candy bar.
Credit: Beth Kimmerle Collection

49

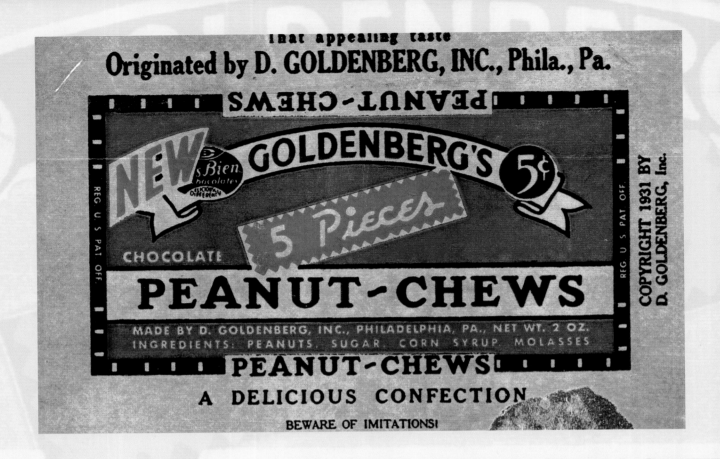

Originated by D. GOLDENBERG, INC., Phila., Pa.

PEANUT-CHEWS

NEW GOLDENBERG'S 5¢

's Bien chocolates DELICIOUSLY DIFFERENT

5 Pieces

CHOCOLATE

REG U S PAT OFF.

REG U S PAT OFF.

COPYRIGHT 1931 BY D. GOLDENBERG, Inc.

PEANUT-CHEWS

MADE BY D. GOLDENBERG, INC., PHILADELPHIA, PA., NET WT. 2 OZ.
INGREDIENTS: PEANUTS, SUGAR, CORN SYRUP, MOLASSES

PEANUT-CHEWS

A DELICIOUS CONFECTION

BEWARE OF IMITATIONS!

During WWI, soldiers tasted their first individually wrapped ration bars. In fact, Goldenberg's Peanut Chews were specifically developed as a World War I ration bar by candy maker Harry Goldenberg. The emergency ration or "E Ration" was a packaged unit of food carried by the soldiers for emergency conditions. It consisted of three cakes of a mixture of beef powder and cooked wheat and three one-ounce chocolate bars. These hardy items were contained in an oval-shaped metal tin that fit conveniently into a soldier's pocket. Needless to say, the chocolate bars proved more popular than beefcakes.

During the war years, many PMCA presidents sent deputies to represent them at the annual convention. In handwritten minutes from wartime meetings, the absent presidents were dismissed for attending to overseas duties, presumably on service.

In July of 1918, The *Confectioners Journal* published a "Roll Of Honor" listing soldiers serving overseas from the confectionery trade. The list, four pages long, opens with "It is doubtful if any other of the great industries of the nation could

Goldenberg's Peanut Chews were developed as a WWI ration and would later become a big hit as a bite-size favorite during movies.
Credit: Just Born

show a longer list of young soldiers drawn from its forces of peace, in proportion to the numbers employed, than that of the confectionery trade." During WWI the *Confectioners Journal* dealt with many wartime issues such as sugar rationing and tin use regulations. The Journal also made sure to recognize and honor soldiers serving from the confection industry.

an Army issue cargo pant pocket. At the request of the army, The Hershey Company developed a chocolate ration that would sustain a soldier who had little nourishment and could be conveniently carried in his pocket without melting. Throughout the war, Hershey turned out a half million bars per day of "Ration D", a huge 4-ounce, 600-calorie chocolate bar. Hershey earned itself five Army-Navy "E" Production Awards for its exceptional contributions to the war effort. In

WWII

It is said that M&M'S were developed after Forest Mars saw soldiers consuming panned candies during the Spanish civil war in the late 1930s. By the 1940s, M&M'S were being enjoyed by American soldiers. They were uniquely packaged in a special cardboard tube that fit directly into

fact, the company's machine shop along with NECCO's in Boston turned out parts for the U.S. military during the war.

Confections included in rations became a profitable business for candy makers and gave companies access to rationed ingredients like sugar, dairy and other raw materials. When home

M&M'S Chocolate Candies were first sold in 1941 and soon became a favorite of American GIs serving in World War II. The cardboard tube packaging was ideal for GI's pants pockets and the candies traveled well in any climate.

A delicious piece of candy
Brightens up the day,
Helps to build morale
In a friendly sort of wa[y]
Helps to make a fighting m[an]
Feel so fine and strong,
And also helps in chasing
All his troubles right alon[g]

from their overseas service, soldiers sought popular wartime rations such as M&M'S, Charms, Tootsie Rolls, Kreem Maid Fudge, Oh Henry! bars and Chiclets.

During the war production of both Hershey's Kisses and Wrigley's gum were temporarily curtailed due to aluminum foil rations. While Hershey remained busy focused on their ration bars, Wrigley developed an advertising

campaign. Pleading with consumers to "Remember This Wrapper," large billboards depicting an image of a Wrigley's Spearmint gum package were plastered across the nation.

While some candy companies were developing new technology to fulfill their wartime contracts, other companies were busy selling candy to raise the spirits of soldiers and loved ones at home. Whitman's shipped chocolate filled tins to troops, some of which

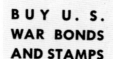

BUY U. S.
WAR BONDS
AND STAMPS

52

included special notes of encouragement written to the men on the front lines by our ladies on the confection lines.

"UNCLE WIGGLY-WINGS" DROPPED A TASTY PAYLOAD

After WWII, the U.S. Air Force was called upon to deliver supplies to war-torn Berlin after Soviet leader Joseph Stalin cut off ground routes to the city. A massive airlift was organized and became the largest humanitarian operation ever undertaken by the U.S. Air Force. More than 2.3 million tons of supplies were flown into the city during the 10-month maneuver.

The American forces dropped goods and cargo necessary to keep Berliners alive, including coal, food, medical supplies, steamrollers, power plant machinery, paper and soap. But the most memorable load seems to have been candy.

While dropping supplies at Berlin's Tempelhof Airport, U.S. pilot Gail Halvorsen met some Berlin children who stood at the fences to marvel at the airborne planes. Touched by their gratitude when he gave them gum, he cajoled his crewmates into pooling their candy rations for the children. For the next several weeks, they dropped their treats to the children, using army-issued handkerchiefs as parachutes and signaling a load by wiggling the plane's wings. A German journalist, who noticed the unique activity, wrote a story about the man the children were calling the "Candy Bomber." Soon children were sending letters to "Uncle Wiggly-Wings" requesting chocolate and American candies. To fulfill the requests, the men on base began donating their candy rations and soon packages of candy, gum, and handkerchiefs arrived from all over the States. Donations of candy from Pennsylvania manufacturers were used to sweeten parachutes.

All told American aircraft dropped more than 23 tons of candy to the children of West Berlin during "Operation Little Vittles," as the operation eventually was called. Colonel Halvorsen went on to win the Cheney Award in 1948 for "...an act of valor, extreme fortitude or self-sacrifice in a humanitarian interest." This simple act became a symbol of hope to the war-torn city and has continued over the years with candy drops in Bosnia, Philippines and Micronesia.

In 2003, a commemorative flight to mark the Berlin Airlift took place and candy once again was parachuted down from the skies. This flight was not flown over Berlin but over the Wright Brothers memorial in North Carolina to honor the progress of the airplane. Donated candy was coordinated by the PMCA.

War Bonds helped the U.S. government finance the war effort. Although the bonds yielded a mere 2.9 percent return after a 10-year maturity, many confectionery companies including Curtiss Candy joined celebrities like Bette Davis and Rita Hayworth to promote their sale.

Thousands save on lunch this tasty way

They know their Baby Ruth

Here's a real way to make your lunches more delightful, and save money too: eat Baby Ruth for dessert. It's delicious and satisfying. A generous tasty treat of dollar-a-pound quality candy for five cents.

Daily, thousands are finding it the most enjoyable dessert they can buy.

Because it is made of purest chocolate, nuts, milk and sugar, dietitians say Baby Ruth makes a light lunch more invigorating than a heavier meal—that it supplies all the extra energy you need for hard work and play. Because you eat less and feel better, it's a healthful way to control your weight.

Baby Ruth is famous for flavor and *guaranteed fresh*. Treat yourself at lunch today. 5c does it.

CURTISS
Baby Ruth
America's Favorite Candy 5¢

© 1928 C. C. Co.

In dainty slices — the popular guest candy of today

CURTIS
CANDY COMPANY, CHICA

OTTO SCHNERING, President

Also makers of Baby Ruth Gum "with that old time Peppermint

MADE IN BILLIONS FOR AMERICA'S MILLIO

CONFECTIONS IN THE 1930s

After WWI, candy making emerged as a top American industry as returning doughboys who had enjoyed candy bars overseas initiated a candy bar boom in the 1920s.

The success of the candy business did not stop with the stock market crash of 1929. Although the business had its share of mergers and bankruptcies, the quickly adapting industry would soon become known as "recession proof." Despite the economic downturn of the 1930s, *Time Magazine* reported that candy sales for the first few months of 1934 were 28 precent better than in 1933. U.S. citizens were eating an average of a pound of candy per person every month.

In 1933, Milton S. Hershey's profits of $4,246,000 went to his Hershey Industrial School and through the Depression, as his profits increased, he graciously enlarged his 5-cent bar for consumers. At the same time, Chicago's Mars, Inc. owned a whopping 20 percent of the candy bar business with their leaders, Milky Way, Snickers and the now obsolete Honey Almond. But during the lean Depression years, candy bars were pricy for many who focused instead on bulk penny candy and purchased long lasting suckers, molasses candies and toffee for value.

When Prohibition ended in 1933, candy makers could again sell candy made with liquor. But some went a little too far when they started marketing their cocktail candy to children. *Time Magazine* reported that some teachers in Brooklyn and Philadelphia began to note their pupils' dull eyes, thick speech and wobbly walk. The easy to obtain, 2-cent cordial candies contained brandy or cognac and a few pieces, supposedly equivalent to a stiff cocktail, were making children drunk. Storeowners were blamed for selling the candy but they said they had purchased the candies from a very mysterious distributor, who left no calling card and was never to return again.

Candy companies used the downturn in the economy to promote the value of a 5-cent candy bar. (Left) A 1928 Curtiss Candy Company advertisement for Baby Ruth. A Luden's advertisement (above) promoting profitability for retailers.

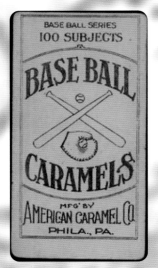

BASE BALL SERIES
100 SUBJECTS

BASE BALL

CARAMELS

MFG' BY
AMERICAN CARAMEL CO.
PHILA., PA.

PITTSBURG

FLYNN PITTSBURG
NEW IN CO

This set consists of pictures of 120 of the
leading
BASE BALL STARS
—of the—
AMERICAN AND NATIONAL LEAGUES
—Made only by—
AMERICAN CARAMEL COMPANY,
LANCASTER AND YORK, PENNA.

The first major set of baseball cards was issued by the
Breisch-Williams Company of Oxford, Pa. in 1903.

CANDY GETS IN THE GAME: BASEBALL CARDS FROM PA CONFECTIONERS

Confectionery companies were among the earliest producers of baseball cards. The very first cards appeared in the 1860s and quickly gained in popularity as marketing tools for promoting brands and connecting with fans of the growing game. The original cards typically featured an image of a player on the front and information about the player along with advertising on the back. As advancements were made in printing and photography, cards began to feature sophisticated images and color artwork. These new techniques created increased demand for the cards and reflected the growing popularity of the game itself.

Pennsylvania confectioners were at the forefront of this new phenomenon and it was the Breisch-Williams Company of Oxford, Pa. that produced the first major set of cards of the new century in 1903. The cards featured black and white photos of players on the front and the text, "One of a hundred and fifty prominent baseball players" on the back. The set was a hit at the time and remains incredibly popular with avid collectors today.

Not to be outdone, the caramel producers of Pennsylvania began issuing cards featuring photo-realistic color artwork of the most popular baseball players. In 1910, the American Caramel Company of Philadelphia issued a set of over 100 players that included such baseball legends as Honus Wagner of the Pittsburgh Pirates and Ty Cobb of the Detroit Tigers. York Caramel Company was another Pennsylvania company that saw the production of baseball cards as a great way to gain customers, and it issued a legendary set in 1927. The York Caramel set was distinguished by its inclusion of players like Babe Ruth, Lou Gehrig and Rogers

Shown in the background is a postcard from the Oxford Confectionery factory in Oxford, Pa. A 1921 set included 20 players with legends like Ty Cobb and Babe Ruth and the individual cards are now traded for thousands of dollars each.

AMERICAN CARAMEL CO.

INCORPORATED 1898

Successors to
P. C. WIEST CO.
Established 1879

LANCASTER CARAMEL CO.
Established 1889

YORK
PENNA.

A V .KUNTZ
623 MAIN STREET
SLATINGTON PA

THE AMERICAN CARAMEL CO., YORK, PA., Hereby Guarantees that each and all Articles mentioned in this
Invoice are not adulterated or misbranded in the Original Unbroken Package, form, nature and composition as packed
and shipped to you within the meaning of the provisions of the Food and Drug Act passed by the Congress of the
United States, and approved June 30, 1906, as amended.
AMERICAN CARAMEL CO.

TER
STRICTLY
30 DA
2% ALLOWE
WITHIN 10 D
DATE OF IN

No.	DATE OF INVOICE	OUR ORDER NO.	YOUR ORDER NO.	SALESMAN	LAST DISC
956	4/27/25	L 749		MAC 534	MAY 7

UNIT	DESCRIPTION		PRICE	AMOUNT	
OX	VERIGOOD 120				
OX	MACAROONS 600				
			62½	13 75	
			63½	12 70	

Received 5/7/25
ACH 4061

58

Hornsby. All of the cards were packaged with a piece of caramel and serious collectors pay a premium if candy scent is still noticeable on the card, indicating that the card was carefully preserved.

Candy and chocolate companies have issued collectible card sets featuring boxers, birds and bicycles; but it is baseball cards that continue to remain popular throughout the years. Cards are now offered at major auction houses and they continue to inspire collectors and inform fans at pretty prices.

Baseball cards serve as reminders of the great history of the game and help to celebrate the roots of our national pastime. Pennsylvania confectionery companies made major contributions in recording some of the earliest moments and celebrating baseball's best players in their own sweet way.

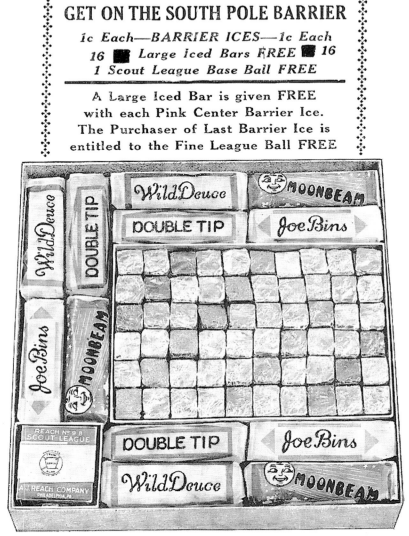

South Pole Barrier Ices

300 Count   1c Each

GET ON THE SOUTH POLE BARRIER
1c Each—BARRIER ICES—1c Each
16 ■ Large Iced Bars FREE ■ 16
1 Scout League Base Ball FREE

A Large Iced Bar is given FREE
with each Pink Center Barrier Ice.
The Purchaser of Last Barrier Ice is
entitled to the Fine League Ball FREE

Each Box Packed Complete
Ready for Display as Illustrated
☞ Packed 30 Boxes to Case
AMERICAN CARAMEL CO., Lancaster, Pa.
A6—2M—4-29

American Caramel was on the forefront of producing baseball card sets but this 1925 invoice shows they also made a variety of candies including macaroons, which cost 2 cents each.
Image: Beth Kimmerle Collection

As confectioners realized the importance of baseball to American lives, they developed baseball cards and included prizes as sales incentives to retailers and consumers alike in their candy.
Credit: Beth Kimmerle Collection

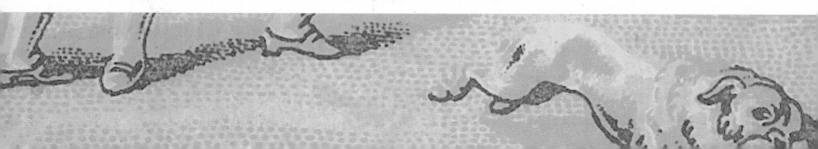

······· *Section 6* ·······

CONFECTIONERY TRADE CARDS

While patronizing your local confectioners, bakery or ice cream parlor around the turn of the 19th century you may have received an advertising card in your parcel, box or bag. Fabulously illustrated with beautiful graphics these "trade cards" may have been inserted into packages at the factory or given away by shopkeepers.

Candy manufacturers and retailers alike used trade cards to show off their wares and they became one of the most popular forms of advertising in the 19th century. Printed on the cards were illustrated scenes that typically featured adorable children, friendly animals, bouquets of flowers and lovely women. New industry and technology was much celebrated at the end of the 19th century and the facilities of candy manufacturers and retailers were often depicted in a grandiose style.

As the availability of presses grew and reduced the costs of printing, advertising materials informing customers about their goods and services developed. The 1876 Centennial Exhibition in Philadelphia provided a premiere opportunity

During the Victorian era, a favorite pastime was collecting small, illustrated business advertising cards. These colorful cards were sometimes pasted into a scrapbook. As people shared their collections with friends and neighbors, they became a powerful advertising medium.

for commercial lithographers to display their products, as well as an opportunity for exhibiting businesses to hand out trade cards promoting their products. By the early 1880s, the color chromolithographed trade card was extremely popular and being distributed widely by businesses ranging from local candy shops to large confection manufacturers.

Trade cards introduced society to the idea of buying factory-made candy or store-bought confections which, until then, had been primarily been made by hand at home. Brand names and trademarks began to appear on cards, inspiring name recognition and continued use of products. Often the colorful cards were issued in themed sets to encourage card collecting and promote repeat purchasing. Trade cards were tremendously appealing and collecting trade cards became a highly fashionable fad in the 1880s. Although the popularity of the trade card peaked by the end of the century as printed magazines

and catalogs gained popularity, they've returned to a valued position today. They've become a meter of industry, past consumer behavior and marketing techniques. Scholars of business history, Americana and graphic design are interested in visually exciting, historical and sought after early business cards.

Trade cards introduced manufactured goods, confectionery and otherwise, that were newly available to American consumers.
Beth Kimmerle Collection

Chapter 3

Production Conference and Expansion 1947-2002

PRODUCTION CONFERENCE: A NEW FORUM

New wartime technology led to exciting innovations within the confection industry but most process and manufacturing technology remained highly confidential, living within the walls of America's disparate candy factories. After the war, members of the PMCA realized the value in shared knowledge and provided a forum via the PMCA Production Conference. The goal of the meeting was to bring confectionery industry people together to discuss technical issues and opportunities in a friendly, frank and non-competitive way. Hans F. Dresel is considered to be the founder of these open forums.

In 1947, the first PMCA Production Conference was held at Lehigh University in Bethlehem. In years following, the event took place during the same week in April and was a 3-day business function dedicated to the technology of candy making. The event, primarily for manufacturers, would start on Tuesday and wrap up by Thursday. Historically, on Wednesday the attendees would take a group picture documenting their presence.

At the first conference in his remarks, PMCA chair and Research Program leader, C. Rudolph Kroekel noted, "I am deeply gratified at the response to our invitation to the confectionery industry to cooperate in this first conference. Its success depends largely upon two factors; the caliber of the conference leaders and their messages, and the response of those who we might call the pupils—those from the production ranks who are attending the conference. I myself am confident that the idea is worthwhile and that our conference will be a success, and sincerely hope that this will be the beginning of a regular program of conferences in our industry."

An early PMCA Production Conference Class.

And a regular conference it was — by the mid-1950s the PMCA Production Conference was held at Franklin & Marshall College in Lancaster and the traditional "Pennsylvania Dutch" dinner held on the opening night of the conference provided a social outlet from the day's lectures, ranging from formulas to flavorings. Classic Dutch dishes like chow chow, shoofly pie, schnitz and knepp, dried corn and whoopie pies were enjoyed in a social setting, sometimes with members donning traditional "Dutch" clothing.

For many years the PMCA also hosted an Annual Meeting, a social event usually held in June that allowed Pennsylvania candy making families an opportunity to visit together. But by the 1960s, the technical Production Conference became PMCA's defining event, providing an organized open forum for the exchange of technical information. As PMCA's membership grew, the conference expanded as an important outlet for candy manufacturers who met yearly, with the goal to continually improve the efficient production of quality chocolate and confectionery. Suppliers were soon invited to join the event, as it was clear they provided not only the tools but also partnerships necessary to a candy maker's survival in the rapidly consolidating industry.

The Production Conference was not all work and no play. In addition to social dinners, the yearly golf outing became an important part of the event. Over the years, it has provided some valuable social time on the golf course before the real courses began.

Pennsylvania has been known for its dairy and milk processing and in 1983 PMCA nodded to the Pennsylvania dairy and farm industries when they introduced the naming of a PMCA "Candy Queen." The PMCA queen took her place alongside the Apple Queen, Potato Queen and, of

Production Conference: technologists who went back to school share knowledge...

It's recess time for technologists who went back to school. L. to r. are: Gibbie Holmberg, of John Sheff-man, Inc. with G. Lloyd Latten, v.p., and J. Durden, Jr., both of McAfee Candy. In second photo, Mat Sholow-ski of Thos. D. Richardson and Charles A. Smylie, v.p. National Licorice listen to A. Rodney Murray, National Philadelphia mgr., describe the program. Next, Joh Kooreman of Penick & Ford, and secy.-treas. of th American Association of Candy Technologists is in rea in front is Bob Krone, of Fritzsche Brothers, conversin with R. B. Esterly, Ludens' v.p. of production. In la photo are, Ed. Meeker, American Sugar, and Fre Moser of Ludens, with J. L. Robinson, president of Jab Burns. The session was part of the three day 13th a nual Production Conference sponsored by the Pennsy vania Manufacturing Confectioners' Association Franklin & Marshall College in Lancaster, Pa.

course, Dairy Queen. The Candy Queen acted as an ambassador to many functions throughout Pennsylvania including the Philadelphia Candy Show, The Farm Show, school visits and AACT meetings. While the Candy Queen concept fizzled in time, the glamorous tiara remains with PMCA as a reminder of bygone regal era of the 1980s.

To this day the famous PMCA "Candy Bag" remains a prized feature of the event. For the attendees of the Production Conference, the bag represents a reward after the days of hard work and learning. PMCA members still look forward to their oversized satchel of candy and are invigorated to leave Hershey with new concepts in their heads and a candy bag in hand.

RESEARCH: INNOVATIONS IN SCIENCE

In 1947, the same year of the premeire Production Conference, a PMCA Research Committee was established in order to provide scientific material for the PMCA meetings. The first Research Committee members included: John Henry, Rudolph Kroeckel, Ira Minter, Hans Dresel, Mark Heidelberger, and Milton Demareth. The original sponsors of the project included: Atlas Chemical Co., Bachman Chocolate Co., De Witt Henry Co., Felton Chemical Co., Heidelberger Confectionery Co.,

Hershey Chocolate Corporation, Minter Brothers, Keppel's Inc., Kroeckel-Ottinger Inc., and Whitman's.

The original research project was undertaken at Leigh University and directed by Dr. H. A. Neville, with much of the research conducted by

Past PMCA President (1979) and former food science director for W.R. Grace Co. and Wilbur Chocolate Co., Silvio Crespo, examines cocoa beans under a microscope.

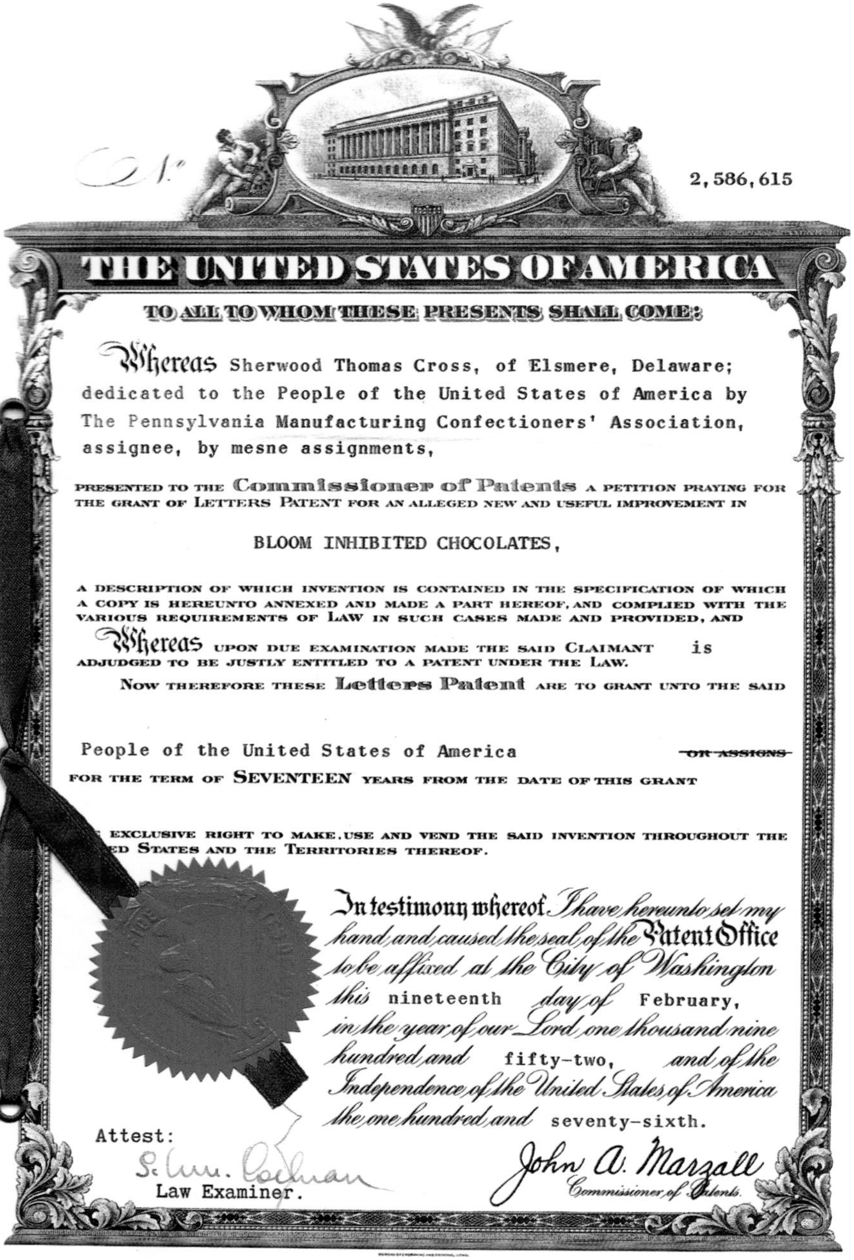

No 2,586,615

THE UNITED STATES OF AMERICA

TO ALL TO WHOM THESE PRESENTS SHALL COME:

Whereas Sherwood Thomas Cross, of Elsmere, Delaware; dedicated to the People of the United States of America by The Pennsylvania Manufacturing Confectioners' Association, assignee, by mesne assignments,

PRESENTED TO THE Commissioner of Patents A PETITION PRAYING FOR THE GRANT OF LETTERS PATENT FOR AN ALLEGED NEW AND USEFUL IMPROVEMENT IN

BLOOM INHIBITED CHOCOLATES,

A DESCRIPTION OF WHICH INVENTION IS CONTAINED IN THE SPECIFICATION OF WHICH A COPY IS HEREUNTO ANNEXED AND MADE A PART HEREOF, AND COMPLIED WITH THE VARIOUS REQUIREMENTS OF LAW IN SUCH CASES MADE AND PROVIDED, AND

Whereas UPON DUE EXAMINATION MADE THE SAID CLAIMANT is ADJUDGED TO BE JUSTLY ENTITLED TO A PATENT UNDER THE LAW.

NOW THEREFORE THESE Letters Patent ARE TO GRANT UNTO THE SAID

People of the United States of America ~~OR ASSIGNS~~

FOR THE TERM OF SEVENTEEN YEARS FROM THE DATE OF THIS GRANT

... EXCLUSIVE RIGHT TO MAKE, USE AND VEND THE SAID INVENTION THROUGHOUT THE ...ED STATES AND THE TERRITORIES THEREOF.

In testimony whereof I have hereunto set my hand and caused the seal of the Patent Office to be affixed at the City of Washington this nineteenth day of February, in the year of our Lord one thousand nine hundred and fifty-two, and of the Independence of the United States of America the one hundred and seventy-sixth.

Attest:

S. Wm. Cochran

Law Examiner.

John A. Marzall

Commissioner of Patents.

On February 19, 1952 PMCA was granted patent number 2,586,615 for Bloom Inhibited Chocolates. It was dedicated to the people of the United States of America.

Dr. Nelson Easton. The program planned to study methods to enlogate the shelf life of chocolate and confectionery products. Research was concentrated on "fat bloom" and the tempering of chocolate. By 1948, Professor Easton was delivering a report at the production conference on specific methods to combat chocolate bloom, thereby extending the shelf life of countless candies and saving PMCA members millions of dollars in wasted product.

That first year, Dr. Stroud Jordan, M.S., Ph.D., author, scholar, research pioneer and an outstanding authority on sugar, was invited to speak at the first PMCA Production Conference. His presentation was titled "Sugar Grades and Their Usage." From the proceedings of the first conference it was described that "[He] was asked some questions regarding the different sizes of crystals in the various grades of granulated sugar which he explained in his usual brilliant manner. The discussion period was enjoyed by all in attendance."

Dr. Stroud Jordan, through his very first lecture and future involvement, helped set standards for PMCA's technical research and for the entire confectionery industry. His talks, books and research inspire other candy technologists and pioneer industry research to this very day.

In 1954, as PMCA funded research moved from Lehigh Universty to Franklin & Marshall College in Lancaster, Pa., Bill Duck began his tenure as official PMCA food scientist and director. Bill was an innovator and pioneer who fabricated his own laboratory with simple hand wrought instruments and immediately commenced research on chocolate bloom, graininess in hard candy and consistency in marshmallow, starch gel candy and caramel.

While with PMCA, Duck patented important research on chocolate fat bloom and tempering. In his 1986 Hans Dresel memorial speech, he modestly referred to the vital work done with his crude setup: "I think we gained some very important information about chocolate from this collection of a metal cup, string, coat hanger wire, and an old basket."

Former PMCA president, board chairman, and PMCA research committee member Jay Musser

was also a vital part of research. A chemical engineer by training, Musser had a long and notable career at Klein Chocolate, now part of M&M Mars in Elizabethtown, Pa. He was a well-known expert in chocolate manufacturing and lent his expertise to PMCA for many years while he acquired a personal research library of note. He stressed the importance of a library for the members of PMCA and many of the books now contained in the PMCA collection are from Musser's personal collection once housed in his home.

Today the PMCA houses an array of confectionery-related books at its offices in Bethlehem, Pa. The library consists of a variety of hard-copy books, historical material, reports and CD-ROMs on various subjects relating to the confectionery industry and collection titles are available on-line to all members. The authors themselves, member companies and industry individuals who have been long-time supporters of PMCA have graciously donated many of the books. The PMCA library is also a repository for theses and reports developed from ongoing confectionery research.

By 1973 the first annual PMCA seminar for research sponsors was held. These seminars are subsequently held every year to discuss any immediate problems, products, and processes affecting the chocolate and confectionery industries.

The seminars help steer the direction of research and provide yet another outlet to understand the collective topics facing all manufacturers. The seminars, now held every three years and hosted in full or part by PMCA, have become a place to understand where to put collaborative efforts and funds for the benefit of all future confectioners. It remains a forum for discussing leading edge research in confectionery science.

Professor Paul S. Dimick was the head of the PMCA's cocoa and chocolate research program for 23 years at Penn State University. His research on flavors, processing and sensory qualities of chocolate have been paramount to PMCA members. Twenty-two students obtained degrees in chocolate and confection under his tutelage. The Penn State University Chocolate and Confectionery program was initiated with support from the PMCA in 1965 and Penn State remains a partner in PMCA research and education. Today, PMCA research partners and grant recipients include many top universities and institutions including an active partnership with University Of Wisconsin at Madison, where industry associations regularly hold confectionery courses.

By 1989, PMCA established a graduate fellowship for confectionery research at Penn State University through an endowment to honor the memory of outstanding past leaders of PMCA. Today, part of the PMCA mission is a commitment to foster the education and training of future technical and manufacturing leaders and talent in the confectionery industry.

PMCA continues to fund major research projects that are pertinent to industry. The resulting studies are available to PMCA members via the library and PMCA published books and articles. Often research results are tailored for practicality to industry applications and presented as a condensed paper and slide presentation at the Annual Production Conference, or at a research symposium.

EDUCATION AND LEARNING: FRESH PRIORITIES

In 1990, the PMCA started its Short Course Program and offered a class on caramel making. In keeping with its primary goal of helping confectioners manufacture better products through education and information, PMCA now offers a series of specialized training classes to both marketing and manufacturing personnel from member companies. The Short Course classes are also open to members of other industry groups such as AACT, NCA, CMA, and RCI and topics have expanded to include a variety of confections from chocolate to chewing gum and starch moulded to hard candy.

Before PMCA Production Conferences and Educational courses, most confectioners learned the craft of candy making through catalogs, books and trial-and-error. Shown here is a mail order book offered in a 1923 *International Confectioner*. For $3, *Rigby's Reliable Candy Teacher* offered 900 candy formulas and recipes.
Image: Beth Kimmerle Collection

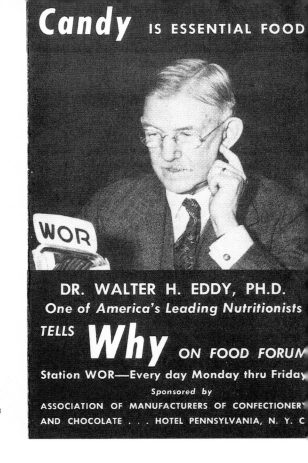

The Short Courses are instructed by industry
practitioners and are meant to provide theoretical
and hands-on training. They are held at the
facilities of confectionery manufacturers or an
approved university facility, and are conducted
by both working industry facilitators and acade-
micians. The PMCA education and training program was designed to create an opportunity for
economical and practical training.

Today the PMCA continues to offer both
research grants and courses in the interest
of furthering the knowledge of science in
confectionery manufacturing.

Candy Is Essential Food; a brochure prepared by
Dr. Walter Eddy, promoting the benefits of candy,
published in 1943. Most likely produced in
response to wartime sugar rationing, the
brochure argues that as candy is used in military rations then thereby it must be "essential"
to the American public too.
Image: PMCA Archives

71

TASTYKAKE

"The Cake That made Mother Stop Bakin'

TASTYKAKE AT PMCA

In 1914, a Pittsburgh baker, Philip J. Baur, and a Boston egg salesman, Herbert T. Morris, went into business in Philadelphia to produce baked goods using farm fresh ingredients. The products were apparently so good that Morris' wife, upon trying a sample, proclaimed they were incredibly "tasty". Thusly, they named their bourgeoning baking business, Tasty Baking Company. At 10-cents each, their Tastykakes went on to be a hugely popular item. By 1918, Tasty Baking was selling $6 million dollars worth of their packaged snack cakes. As the company grew, they proceeded to expand their bakery goods business selling everything from cupcakes to pies. Tasty Baking was once a regional operation, selling its products only in the Philadelphia metropolitan area. The company now distributes its products in several states on the East Coast. Especially for many Philadelphians, Tasty Baking Company led a "comfort food" revolution with their individually packaged, well-priced, lunchbox-sized pastries. While Tastykake has been a long-time sponsor of the Philadelphia Phillies broadcasts, many long-time PMCA members remember the Tastykakes sponsorship of coffee breaks at PMCA conferences held at Franklin & Marshall College.

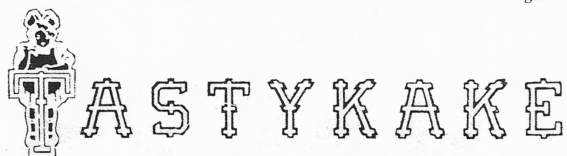

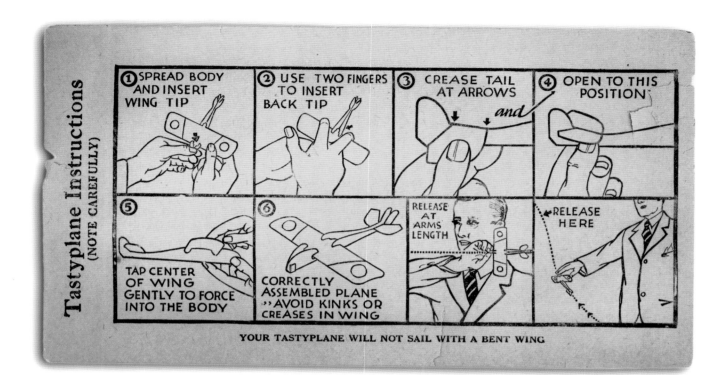

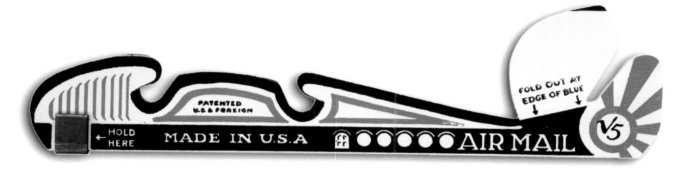

Tastykake's lunch box pastries ran a 1930s promotion
for a flying airplane or Tastyplane.

Chapter 4

Today and Our Future
(2003-2007)

Today PMCA is an active volunteer-run organization known for bringing the industry together through cooperation on issues that otherwise may be considered confidential and competitive. In the early years, as Pennsylvania area confectionery companies began to emerge and grow, the association was formed in an effort for seven distinct companies to work together to instill a sense of ethics in the industry. Later, in the 1940s, PMCA would begin to offer their now historic yearly Production Conference providing a forum for candy makers to discuss the science behind the production of their confections. Today, with the addition of a permanent office, international members and its programming of industry wide respected meetings and research, PMCA has become more than a simple trade organization, it has become an institution.

The PMCA 100 Year Anniversary chocolate bar was given away at the 2007 Production Conference. One special bar contained a "Golden Ticket" offering the winner complimentary attendance to the PMCA Gala Event in October 2007.

Today
THE MISSION OF THE PMCA IS:

1. *To provide an open forum for the free exchange of information*

PMCA's Annual Production Conference, held each April in Hershey, Pennsylvania, provides an open forum for the exchange of technical information. Candy manufacturers and their suppliers meet with the goal to continually improve the manufacturing quality of candy by listening to technical presentations, by networking to explore industry issues with other manufacturers, and by viewing supplier exhibits. The technical papers presented are published as the Proceedings in print and in electronic form. Registration is open to manufacturers and suppliers in the confectionery and related industries.

2. *To promote and direct basic and applied scientific research*

PMCA's Research Committee directs basic and applied scientific research in the science of chocolate and confectionery at several leading universities. The PMCA has endowed a graduate fellowship in Confectionery Food Science at Pennsylvania State University.

3. *To educate and train confectionery technical personnel worldwide*

PMCA's program of Short Courses in Confectionery Technology offers unique opportunities for member companies to educate and train their technical and manufacturing personnel through courses of three to four days in length. Usually three to four courses are offered annually, covering a broad range of processes with topics continually rotated.

The inside story of **Ambrosia**
FOOD OF THE GODS

Ice Cream Coatings

Ambrosia
BAKING CHOCOLATE

AMBROSIA CHOCOLATE CAKE

Cream 6 tablespoons shortening, add ¾ cup granulated sugar gradually and mix well. Add 2 egg yolks, well beaten and blend. Sift 2 cups sifted cake or pastry flour with 4 teaspoons baking powder and ½ teaspoon salt. Add to the shortening mixture alternately with 1 cup milk mixed with 1 teaspoon vanilla. Beat 2 egg whites until almost stiff, then add ½ cup granulated sugar and beat again until stiff. Fold into cake mixture, then turn the batter into two greased and floured 9 inch layer cake pans. Bake for 25-30 min. in moderate oven of 375° F. Remove. Cool. Fill and frost with Ambrosia Chocolate Icing.

AMBROSIA CHOCOLATE ICING

Melt 2½ squares Ambrosia Baking Chocolate with 2 tablespoons butter. Add 2 cups confectioners' sugar and ½ teaspoon salt. Stir until lumpy. Add sufficient cream or top milk (about 5 tablespoons) to make smooth. Add 1 teaspoon vanilla. Mix well and spread on cake. Makes enough icing for filling, top and sides of 9 inch 2 layer cake.

8 OUNCES NET WEIGHT

© 1934

MANUFACTURED BY

AMBROSIA CHOCOLATE CO., MILWAUKEE, WIS.

AMBROSIA BAKING CHOCOLATE

AMBROSIA BAKING CHOCOLATE

**AMBROSIA PREMIUM
BAKING CHOCOLATE**

ONE HALF POUND NET WEIGHT

THE ENGLISH CHOCOLATE-HOUSE

Chapter 5

Our Members: Manufacturers

Section 1

*Those members listed in bold are PMCA Centennial Sponsors

Adams & Brooks, Inc.

ADM Cocoa

American Licorice

The Annapolis Chocolate Co. Inc.

Ann's House of Nuts

Anthony-Thomas Candy Co.

Asher's Chocolates

Askinosie Chocolate, LLC

Barkus Chocolates

Barry Callebaut Canada

Barry Callebaut USA LLC

Bear Creek Operations

Blommer Chocolate Co.

Bloomer Candy Company

Blue Bell Creameries, L.P.

Bochner Confections, Inc.

Brookside Foods Ltd.

Brown & Haley

Cadbury Schweppes

Cargill Cocoa & Chocolate

Beginning in 1953, Amby the cocoa bean with his scepter of nibs (top) was an excellent salesman for Ambrosia's line of ice cream flavorings. Ambrosia Chocolate Company baking chocolate packaging from 1934 (bottom) gave customers a recipe for cake and icing. Image Courtesy: ADM Cocoa

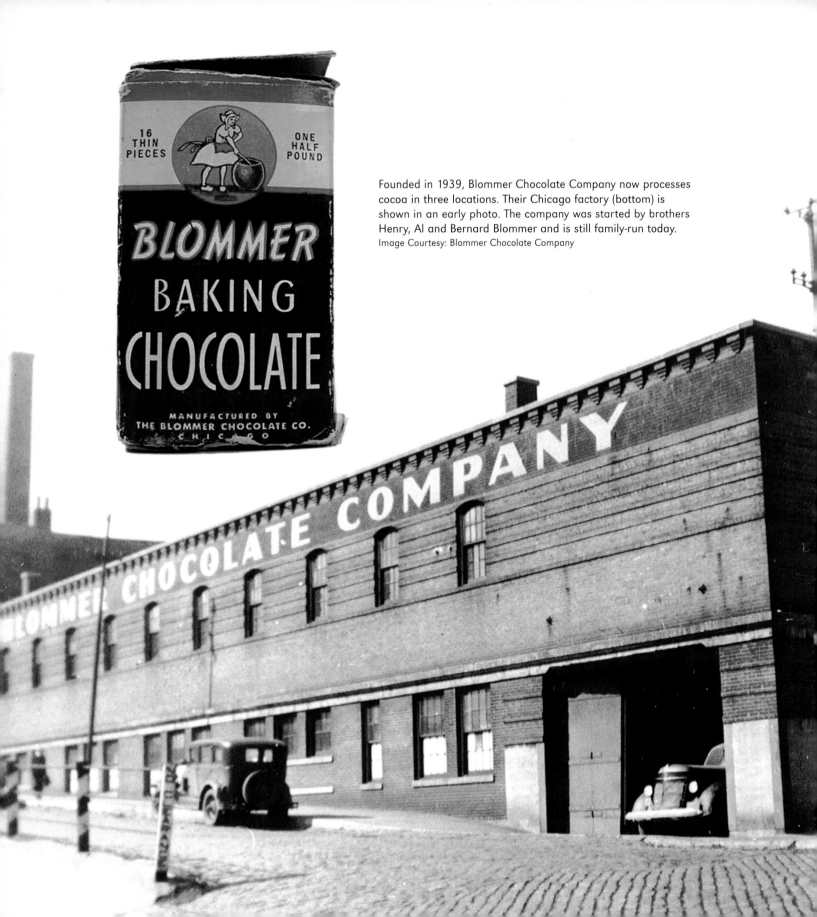

Founded in 1939, Blommer Chocolate Company now processes cocoa in three locations. Their Chicago factory (bottom) is shown in an early photo. The company was started by brothers Henry, Al and Bernard Blommer and is still family-run today.
Image Courtesy: Blommer Chocolate Company

The staff of the Bloomer Candy Company is shown outside the company storefront in Zanesville, Ohio (top) in an early photo. A customer invoice (left) from the year 1885 shows that payment was received in full and one box of chocolate drops was $1. Four generations later, the company is still a family owned business operating part of their chocolate production from the original building on Third Street in downtown Zanesville, Ohio. Finished in 1901, this building was the first in Zanesville to have DC Lighting and an elevator.
Image Courtesy: Bloomer Candy Company

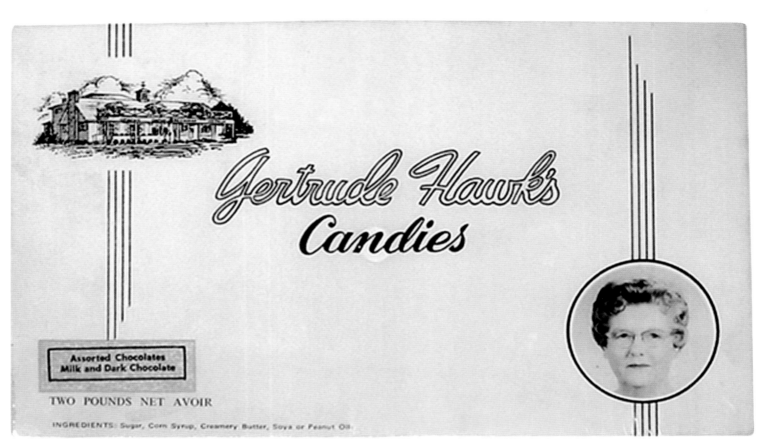

Carlyle Cocoa Company	Elmer Candy Corporation
Cherrydale Farms, Inc.	Ferrara Pan Candy Company Inc.
The Chocolate Doctor	Frankford Candy & Chocolate Co.
Chocolate Potpourri Ltd.	Ganong Bros Limited
Chris Candies, Inc.	Gardner's Candies
Chukar Cherry Company	Georgia Nut Co.
The Classic Caramel Company/Lukas	**Gertrude Hawk Chocolates**
Confections, Inc.	Ghirardelli Chocolate Co.
Classic Pharmaceuticals LLC	Gimbal's Fine Candies
Columbia International Food Products Inc.	Good Foods S.A.
Costas Candies	Granite State Candies LLC
Cream Factory, CA	Green River Chocolates
Daffin's, Inc.	Guan Chong Cocoa Snd. Bhd.
Dagoba Organic Chocolate	Guittard Chocolate Co.
Dolle's Candyland, Inc.	**The Hershey Company**
ECOM Cocoa Atlantic USA, Inc.	Jelly Belly Candy Company

n 1936, Gertrude Hawk started her business in the kitchen of her small home in the Bunker
Hill section of Scranton, Pa. A classic 2-pound box of Gertrude Hawk's candies (top) features a
ameo photo of the company founder. They've grown from a small single location confectioner
o a candy company with over seventy retail stores and several wholesale divisions.
nage Courtesy: Gertrude Hawk Chocolates

CHOCOLATE and COCOA
NOURISHING FOODS

Harvesting Cacao Pods

The cultivated cacao tree grows to a height of twenty-five feet, has large leaves and differs from our fruit trees in that the cacao pods, which are the fruit of the tree, grow on its trunk and main branches. At almost any time of the year it is possible to see the small bright red blossoms, the growing pods and the ripened fruit all present on the tree. The unripe pods are dark green, but as they mature, pass through the successive stages of yellow, orange, red and finally dark maroon. The yield of the trees averages twenty pods weighing a pound each. These are removed by means of a sharp knife attached to the end of a long pole called a podadera, inasmuch as the tree is not strong enough to bear climbing.

Removing Beans From Pod

Cacao pods are from eight to twelve inches in length and from two to five inches in diameter. They are cut open with a small curved knife manipulated by a neat turn of the wrist. Within are found twenty to forty white beans surrounded by a mucilaginous pulp. In English speaking countries the bean is commonly called—cacao.

Upon removal from the pod, the beans are spread out to undergo a fermentation process, which changes the color from white to brownish red. After curing and drying, the beans are placed in large jute bags and are ready for shipment.

Roasting Cocoa Beans

When received in the modern chocolate factory, cocoa beans are first cleaned by being passed over a series of vibrating screens through which fall undersize beans and foreign substances, such as small twigs and stones. Strong air currents aid in the cleaning operations which precede the roasting process. The latter takes place in revolving drums through which air heated to a temperature of more than 300° F. is drawn. This process facilitates later removal of the shells from the beans, removes moisture and develops the color and flavor of the edible portions.

Milling or Grinding Cocoa Nibs

Removal of the shells results in the cracking of the kernels into small angular fragments called nibs. This material—the "meat" of the bean—is ground by being passed through milling machines which consist of three sets of steel encased granite burr stones which revolve at a rapid rate. The friction heat generated by the grinding process causes the cocoa butter, making up more than half of the nibs, to melt, thus producing a smooth free-flowing chocolate liquor, the basis of all forms of chocolate.

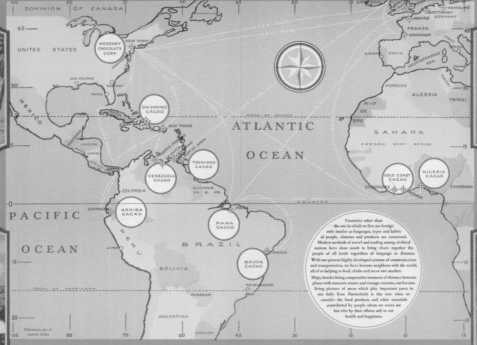

Countries other than the one in which we live are foreign only insofar as languages, types and habits of people, climates and products are concerned. Modern methods of travel and trading among civilized nations have done much to bring closer together the people of all lands regardless of language or distance.

With our present highly developed systems of communication and transportation, we have become neighbors with the world, all of us helping to feed, clothe and serve one another.

Maps, besides being comparative measures of distance between places with romantic names and strange customs, can become living pictures of areas which play important parts in our daily lives. Particularly is this true when we consider the food products and other essentials contributed by people whom we never see but who by their efforts add to our health and happiness.

Manufacturing Cocoa Powder

The most popular form of chocolate for beverage purposes is the familiar cocoa powder. Its preparation involves the reduction of the amount of fat in the chocolate liquor and is accomplished in huge hydraulic presses. The chocolate liquor is conveyed to these heavy duty machines and subjected to the enormous pressure of 6,000 pounds per square inch. Thus a portion of the cocoa butter, a pale yellow fat when warm, is expressed, leaving behind the cocoa cakes which then are cooled and sifted into a fine, soft, rich brown powder.

Producing Wholesome Milk

Few foods require as much care in production and thorough sanitation as does milk, for vitally important are these factors that on them depend entirely whether or not it be fit for human consumption. In the modern dairy, strictest attention is given to the isolated countries to attain the high standards of cleanliness demanded in the production of fine quality milk chocolate.

Pure milk is an excellent source of protein, fat, and carbohydrate, the dietary elements which supply to the body its necessary fuel. It is also rich in mineral matter and contains several of the most important vitamins.

Manufacturing Milk Chocolate

Milk chocolate is a combination of chocolate, whole milk solids, sugar, and cocoa butter. Pure granulated sugar and fresh creamy whole milk are first combined in huge concentrating kettles where most of the water in the milk is removed. The viscous mass produced is placed in mixers with chocolate liquor from the milling machines. This mass turns to a powder, but with the addition of cocoa butter becomes a smooth pasta in which state the solid particles are reduced to microscopic size by steel rollers. The final smoothing and flavor developing operation takes place in large vats equipped with granite rollers under which the chocolate passes continuously for six hours finally acquiring its desired velvety texture and delicate flavor.

Moulding Chocolate Bars

For convenience chocolate is made in various forms, the most popular of which is the chocolate bar. This is accomplished by special machinery where the temperature of the chocolate is carefully watched to insure a glossy appearance, proper body, and a fine fine texture, all of which are indicative of high quality chocolate.

The moulded bars are delivered to wrapping machines, where under the most sanitary methods they are carefully wrapped and protected, then placed in containers which are completely sealed. The boxed chocolate is kept in the cool controlled stock rooms where the temperature and humidity do not vary out the year.

A CACAO POD
ACTUAL SIZE

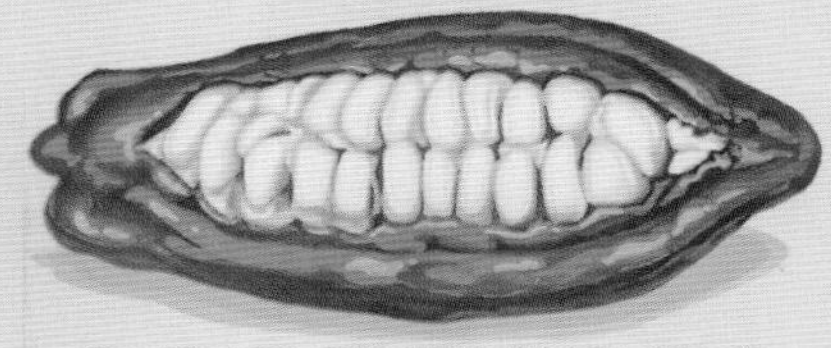

CACAO POD SHOWING COCOA BEANS
ACTUAL SIZE

COCOA BEANS
Roasted cacao beans from which are obtained chocolate and cocoa, are rich brown in color. The beans are covered with a protecting shell or husk which must be cracked and removed to obtain the kernels inside.

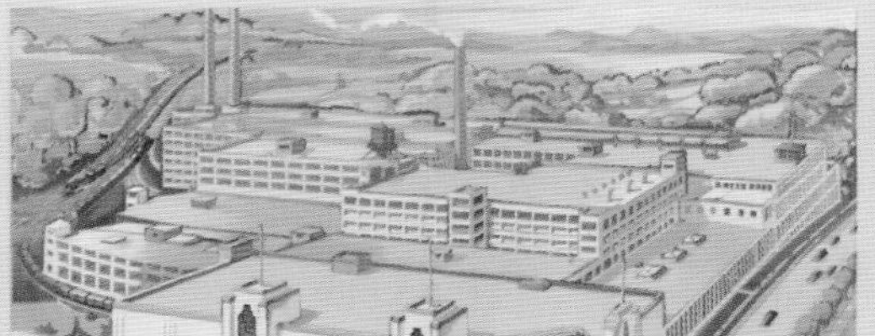

COCOA NIBS
When the outer cover or husk has been removed from cacao beans, nearly tasteless remain. These kernels are cracked and the eye or germ, similar to that in peanuts, is removed. The cracked or broken pieces of natural raw chocolate are called nibs.

COCOA POWDER

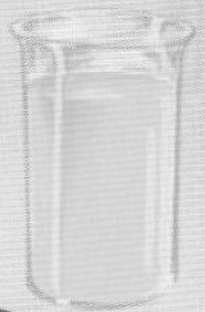

COCOA BUTTER

HERSHEY'S
5¢ MILK CHOCOLATE 5¢

HERSHEY'S BREAKFAST COCOA

HERSHEY'S
Milk Chocolate with ALMONDS 5¢

CHOCOLATE LIQUOR
BAKING AND DRINKING CHOCOLATE

The Story of Cacao
The History of Cocoa

THE story of cacao is one of the most interesting in the world. Long before the discovery of America it was cultivated and used as a food by the Aztecs, the aborigines of Central America. When Christopher Columbus reached the New World, he learned of cacao and took back to Spain a few beans as curios, though he knew nothing of their food value.

A few years later, in 1528, when Cortez of Spain invaded Mexico, the real value of cacao was discovered. The importance of cocoa beans to the Aztecs may be judged by the fact that they were used as a means of exchange, in other words, as money. When Cortez returned to Spain he brought back news of a drink that was entirely unknown in Europe. The drink was called "chocolatl" and was in common use among the Aztecs. From this word came the name "chocolate" so well known to us. The term "cocoa" is derived from "cacao" and is almost universally used in English-speaking countries to designate the seed of the cacao tree.

When Cortez first entered Mexico, the emperor, Montezuma, entertained him and his followers at a banquet at which the only beverage was chocolate flavored with vanilla and other spices, whipped to a froth and served cold. This beverage must have been somewhat similar to our present day chocolate soda. Montezuma drank no other beverage than chocolate. It was served to him in golden goblets and after each one was drained it was thrown into the lake that surrounded his palace. At one feast he emptied fifty goblets while his guards and attendants consumed two thousand goblets.

The Aztecs knew of the nourishing quality of chocolate. During the periods of feasting they would spend all day and the greater part of the night at games of endurance and dancing, with chocolate as their only food. After Cortez introduced cocoa into Spain it soon became very popular although the Spaniards endeavored to keep its preparation a secret. In 1606 it became known in Italy, whence it spread to Austria and was introduced in France by Anne, upon her marriage to Louis XIII.

Chocolate houses became popular in both England and Germany in the middle of the seventeenth century. Spain controlled the world source of cacao and gained great wealth from its sale. So high a price was maintained that the beverage was beyond the reach of any but the most wealthy.

Today chocolate and cocoa are within the reach of everyone and modern scientific opinion almost unanimously awards chocolate an important place in a balanced diet.

The Lands of Cacao
The Geography of Cocoa

IN the days of Columbus a voyage to what is now known as America was a world conquest. Today all the world is closely knit, so improved are the means of transportation and communication. West Africa, South America, Central America, the United States, Europe, and all the world are akin and depend upon each other for many of the things needed in their daily life.

Many products used throughout the world are grown in the tropics where there is little climatic change. Rubber, coffee, dates and figs, palm oil (the basis for many of the soaps upon which we depend for cleanliness), hard woods such as mahogany, ebony and teak, and a host of other things have their origin in the lands of hot sunshine. One of the principal products—the energy food of which the world consumes 500,000 tons a year—is the cocoa bean from which chocolate and cocoa are derived.

In South and Central America, the West and East Indies, and in West Africa, thousands of acres are given over to the cultivation of cacao. The villages or settlements on the West Coast of Africa, from which a large quantity of the finest cocoa comes, are rather primitive. Lagos, a province of Southern Nigeria, is about the size of South Carolina. The principal port is the Capital City also named Lagos, with a population of 126,000. It is a very unhealthful country for white people, and most of the cacao plantations are owned by native cultivators. A shifting sandbar makes the entrance into Lagos Harbor difficult and the boats which transport the cacao to Europe and America generally anchor not less than two miles from shore.

Just the opposite is the rule in South and Central America. There, a high degree of culture and civilization exists. Rio de Janeiro in Brazil is one of the great cities of the world and has a population of over two millions. In area, Brazil is larger than the United States. It has large seaports and from these many ships bearing cocoa go to all quarters of the world.

Ecuador, which produces one-fifth of the world's supply of cacao, is equally modern. These countries and the tropical states in Central and South America, together with numerous islands in the West Indies, comprise the sources of cacao in the Western Hemisphere.

Though the quantities produced are not large, some of the world's finest cocoa comes from the East Indies. The islands of Java, Ceylon and Samoa deserve full praise for their production of cacao beans unsurpassed in quality and excellent flavor.

HERSHEY CHOCOLATE CORPORATION—HERSHEY, PA. U.S.A.

LITHO. IN U.S.A.

Joyva Corporation

Just Born, Inc.

K.C. Confectionery Limited

Kargher Corporation

KCS Creations, LLC

Kerry Sweet Ingredients

Lake Champlain Chocolate Co.

Lindt & Sprüngli (USA) Inc.

Linette Quality Chocolates

Long Grove Confectionery

M&M Mars

Madelaine Chocolate Novelties

Malley's Chocolates

Maxfield Candy Co.

Mayfield Confections Inc.

Melster Candies

Moonstruck Chocolate Company

Morinaga & Co., Ltd.

Morley Brands LLC

Munson's Chocolates

Nancy's Homemade Fudge, Inc.

Nestle Plant

Nestle R&D Center, Inc. Marysville

Niagara Chocolates/Sweetworks

R.M. Palmer Company

Parmalat

Peerless Confection Company

Philadelphia Candies, Inc.

Polyol Innovations, Inc.

Pulakos, Inc.

QA Products, Inc.

Quigley Manufacturing, Inc.

This 1944 chart for Hershey's did more then just sell chocolate. It also gave lessons in geography, chocolate history, and educated customers n the many steps it takes to process cacao into chocolate bars.
mage Courtesy: The Hershey Archives

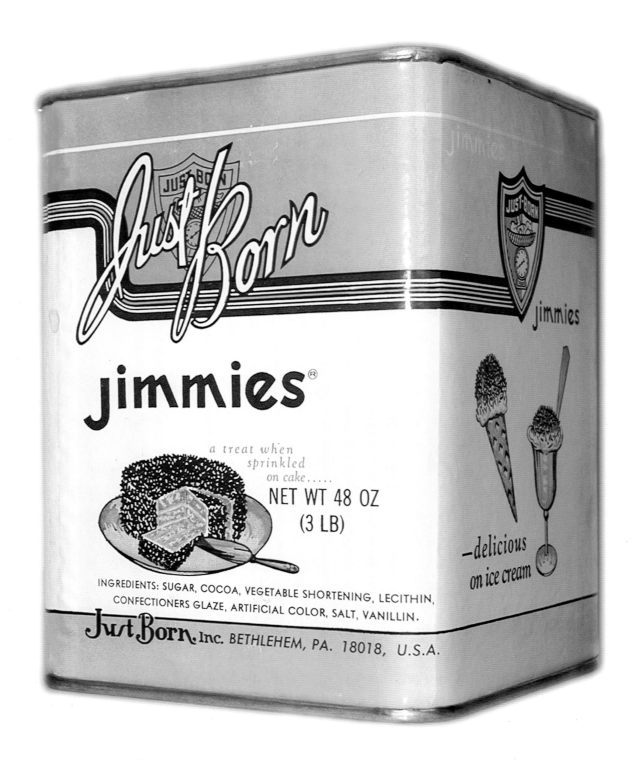

Founder of Just Born, Sam Born was a candy entrepreneur and inventor. In 1916 Born was given the keys to the city of San Francisco for inventing a machine that mechanically inserted sticks into lollipops. Chocolate Jimmies, or sprinkles, used on confections, cookies, and ice cream, were invented at Just Born.

In 1930, Frank Mars introduced a new bar (top) consisting of peanuts, caramel, peanut butter nougat, and milk chocolate. He called it "Snickers" after a family horse and sold it for a nickel. It has become the best-selling chocolate bar of all time. The 3 Musketeers Bar (bottom) followed in 1932 and originally contained individual mini bars of vanilla, strawberry, and chocolate nougat. Since 1945, however, the bars have been made with chocolate nougat only.

Image Courtesy: M&M Mars

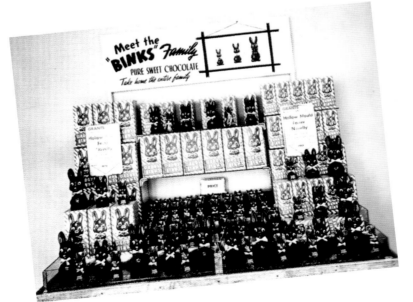

Roger's Chocolates Ltd.

Romolo Chocolates

Seattle Chocolates

See's Candies, Inc.

Sorbee International, Ltd.

Spangler Candy Co.

Splendid Chocolates Limited

Stutz Candy Company, Inc.

Sucesores Pedro Cortes, Inc.

Sweet Candy Company

Sweet Productions Ltd.

Tastysnack Quality Foods Inc.

Thompson Brands, LLC

The Topps Company

Jacques Torres Chocolate

Traverse Bay Confections

Tropical Temptations

United Cocoa Processor

Universal Blanchers-Seabrook Ingredients

Vande Walle's Candies, Inc.

Waggoner Chocolates

The Warrell Corporation

Wolfgang Candy Co.

World's Finest Chocolate

Wm. Wrigley, Jr. Company

Zachary Confections, Inc.

S. Zitner Company

Classic advertising from the R.M. Palmer Company shows their whole "Binks" family of hollow moulded chocolate rabbits. These chocolate bunnies have been delighting children and adults alike since they were first introduced for Easter in 1948. Image Courtesy: R.M. Palmer Company

A 1918 United States Food Administration Poster promoting the use of corn syrup, starch and oils. Federal ration programs were first implemented during World War I and helped to educate citizens about food shortages and sacrificing of ingredients. In 1918, the US production of corn was 3 million bushels. At that time, most was used as feed-grain, with only a small percentage for human consumption.
Image: Library Of Congress

········ *Section 2* ·······

OUR MEMBERS: SUPPLIERS

INGREDIENTS

Early candy making ingredients were basic components that almost all confectioners used. Sugar, butter, cream, nuts and perhaps a little color or natural flavor were the common ingredients that went into most candies. What differentiated a candy was not so much what was in it but how long it was cooked.

In its early years, chocolate was primarily reserved for use in drinking beverages. However, around the late 1800s chocolate would become an important ingredient as manufacturers were able to extract its natural cocoa butter and use cocoa powder in various applications. Chocolate became a more versatile ingredient and confectioners could use it either as flavor or on its own as an ingredient or coating. Today chocolate is a common ingredient in confections like chocolate bars and candy and is also widely used in beverages, baked goods and ice cream. Chocolate is now considered one of the top food flavors in the world.

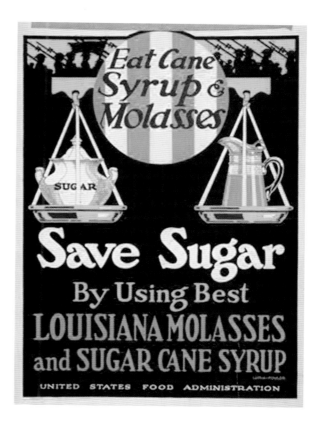

Cane sugar, once expensive and reserved for aristocracy became mass produced and less expensive by the 1800s. Originally from the Pacific Islands, sugar use spread throughout India and Asia and would land in the mouths of Europeans via their crusading Christians. First primarily used as a medicine and then later a spice and preservative during the Middle Ages, the commodity of refined cane sugar was soon equated with luxury, wealth and power.

A 1918 United States Food Administration Poster promoting consumer use of molasses and cane syrup rather than refined sugar. Food manufacturers using sugar were dealt with more strictly than private individuals. During WWI, every business using sugar purchased its supply with certificates obtained from the Federal Food Administrators. Makers of "less essential" food products received a small percentage of what they normally used before the war. Soft drink and candy manufacturers got rationed 50 per cent and ice cream makers 75 per cent.

Image: Library Of Congress

SUPPLIER COMPANIES

*Those members listed in bold are
Centennial Sponsors*

A.M.P. ROSE
A.M. Todd Company
AarhusKarlshamn USA
AarhusKarlshamn Denmark A/S
Aasted-Mikroverk, LTD
Aberco Inc.
ACH Food Companies, Inc.
ACMA G.D.
ADM
Admix, Inc.
Ajinomoto USA Inc.
Aledco Inc.
American Chocolate Mould, Inc.
Amerivap Systems
Ammeraal Beltech Inc.
ARDE Barinco, Inc.
A.R. Arena Products, Inc.
ARLA Foods Ingredients, Inc. No. America
Aspecialtybox.com
The Austin Company
AZO Incorporated
Bainbridge Associates, L.L.C.
Baker Perkins
Balchem Encapsulates
Balsu USA, Inc.
Bariatrix Nutrition
Bartek Ingredients, Inc.
GW Barth AG
BASF Corporation
Bauermeister, Inc.

Just one taste had Europeans seeking the warm climates that could grow the sugarcane plant. By the 17th century, sugar production in the tropical Americas had become the world's largest and most lucrative industry. As Europeans established efficient sugar plantations on the larger Caribbean islands, prices fell drastically. Finally, when processes to refine beet sugar were introduced in the 19th century in Europe, many were able to begin enjoying the taste of something sweet. At first most European sugar went into sweetening beverages like tea and coffee but sugar would soon open up a world of original and affordable confections and chocolates.

When the first manufacture of refined corn syrup occurred in 1882, it was a big event in the human quest for sweetness. Throughout the early 1900s, scientists continued to make advancements in processing cornstarch into corn syrup at the same time that farmers were improving crop yields. As corn syrup was refined and improved, confection manufacturers began to see it as a homegrown, low-cost alternative to sugar. After the first commercial introduction of high fructose corn syrup in 1967, use of the product grew exponentially. The ability of corn syrup to inhibit the crystallization of sugar, to keep products moist, and to inhibit spoilage are all factors in its widespread adoption throughout the confections industry during the 1970s and 1980s.

EQUIPMENT

An early candy kitchen would contain copper kettles, a marble slab, wooden spoons and an open stove as the primary tools necessary to make confections. As candy grew more sophisticated and available so did the equipment to make it.

Thomas Mills Brothers in Philadelphia, Pa. became known for their custom fabricated machines made specifically for bakers and confectioners. Started in 1864, they served confectioners, bakers and the bourgeoning ice cream business with cutters, rollers, moulds, mixers and starch boards. By the 1920s their catalog was

Chocolate making machinery engraving
from a 1920s Thomas Mills catalog
Catalog Courtesy: Frank Friedwald

Bedemco, Inc.
Bell Flavors & Fragrances, Inc.
Bemis Flexible Packaging
Berndorf Belt Technology USA
Blue Diamond Growers
BOC Gases
Robert Bosch Corporation
Bosch Sapal, S.A.
Bosch Sigpack Systems, AG
Bottom Line Process Technologies, Inc.
The Boyd Company, Inc.
Bradman Lake
Bremeer Foods
BS&B Safety Systems, L.L.C.
Buhler, Inc.
Butter Buds Food Ingredients
California Dried Plum Board
California Natural Products
I.P. Callison & Sons
Candy & Snack Business
Candy Industry
Caotech B.V.
Cargill Confectionery Ingredients
Cargill, Inc., DSO Unit
Carle & Montanari USA, Inc.
Carmi Equipment Company
Carmi Flavor & Fragrance Co., Inc.
Carmi Flavor & Fragrance Co., Canada
Catty Corporation
Cavanna Packaging USA, Inc.
Centerchem, Inc.
Charabot & Cie.
Charabot Inc.
Chefmaster
ChocoVision Corp.

No. 1 IMPROVED CANDY MIXER

WITH COPPER STEAM JACKET TILTING KETTLE

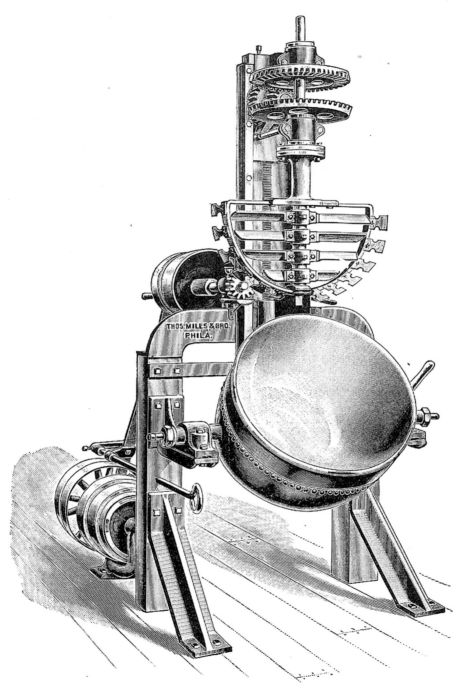

Fig. 483

thick not only with machines but with a page of medals they had won at various exhibitions where their innovative candy making machines were proudly displayed.

Union Confectionery Machinery, founded by Abraham Greenberg, started by selling used and refurbished equipment in New York City in 1912. The Greenberg Family then bought National Equipment in the 1930s and expanded their business to include custom fabricated machines. The international company is now in its fourth generation of ownership by the Greenberg family.

As confectioners had special recipes, often times equipment companies would customize a machine for a unique business. Equipment companies would eventually become partners with confectioners designing their kitchens and machines and becoming keepers of some of the best-kept industry secrets, a confectioner's confidential recipes. Many equipment companies custom build just about anything candy or chocolate which a marketing or R&D department can dream up.

The first European chocolate moulds came to America from Anton Reiche of Dresden, Germany around the turn of the century. Americans were familiar with toy candy moulds for hard candy but as they made progress in chocolate making, specialty novelty moulds

Candy Mixer engraving from a from a 1920s Thomas Mills catalog.
Catalog Courtesy: Frank Friedwald

Chr. Hansen, Inc.
Ciranda, Inc.
CL&D Digital
Clasen Quality Coatings, Inc.
W.A. Cleary Products
Cocotech, Inc.
Colloides Naturels, Inc.
Colorcon
Comax Flavors
Concord Foods Inc. Oringer Division
Constantia Multifilm
F. D. Copeland & Sons Limited
Corn Products U.S.
C-P Flexible Packaging
CP Kelco
Creative Food Ingredients, Inc.
Cremer North America
Crosio & Associates, Inc.
Dairy Farmers of America, Inc.
Danisco USA, Inc.
Danisco Sweeteners
David Michael & Co.
Davisco Foods International, Inc.
Debelis Corporation
Deibel Laboratories
Del-Val Food Ingredients
DESMI Inc./ROTAN Pumps
Diamond Foods, Inc.
Dietrich's Milk Products LLC
Dietrich's Specialty Processing, LLC
Doboy, Inc.
Domino Specialty Ingredients
Draiswerke, Inc.
Driam USA, Inc.
DSM Nutritional Products, Inc.

PATTERNS FOR BOILED SUGAR TOYS

The making of sugar toys or clear toy candies is a Pennsylvania German tradition that dates back to the 18th century. Children were given the candies for holidays and special occasions. They would play with the candy as a toy and then the toy would be washed "clear" with water to make it ready for consumption. When made properly, clear toy candy was a "clear" or perfect representation of the intricate people and animal moulds that were used to produce them. Shown here are various clear toy patterns available from a 1920s Thomas Mills Brothers candy equipment catalog. Clear toy candy making machines were modeled on the printing press and used interchangeable patterned rollers to stamp out different candy shapes.

Catalog Courtesy: Frank Friedwald

Here are a few of the latest designs of the famous
"REICHE" Chocolate Moulds

T. C. Weygandt Co.
Sole Agents for U. S. A. and Canada
248-A West Broadway   New York, N. Y.

would become popular with boutique confectioners. Ornamental moulded chocolates from simple bars to impressive animal shapes became an elaborate way to both consume and brand chocolate.

While cooking equipment and methods have not changed much throughout the history of candy

This advertisement from a 1928 *Confectioners Journal* shows the latest designs of Anton Reiche chocolate moulds. Friedrich Anton Reiche (1845-1913) of Dresden, Germany, was a tinsmith who taught himself to make chocolate and ice cream moulds. His factory, established in 1870, supplied intricately sculpted metal moulds to confectioners all over the world. Reiche moulds were exported to the U.S. from 1885 (with a brief interruption during WWI) until the late 1930s. During WWII, the city of Dresden and the Reiche factory were almost completely demolished by Allied bombing in February 1945.
Image: Beth Kimmerle Collection

Hampton Farms
Hazelnut Council
Hilliard's Chocolate System
Holland Sweetener North America, Inc.
Hosokawa Bepex GmbH
Hosokawa Confectionery & Bakery
Hosokawa Ter Braak
Hydro-Thermal Corporation
IFF
Ilapak, Inc.
Imperial Sugar Company
Industrial Food Ingredients Co., Inc.
Innovia Films, Inc.
International Fiber Corporation
The International Food Network, Inc.
International Foodcraft Corp.
Stephen Izzi Trucking & Rigging, Inc.
Jacob Tubing L.P.
Jeffery Associates
Jennings Associates, Inc.
John Sheffman, Inc.
Jordon Box Company
Jungbunzlauer Inc.
Kantner Ingredients
KDM Foodsales, Inc.
The Kellogg Company
Kerry Americas
Kerry Bioscience
E. Klein Associates
Klikloc-Woodman
Kline Process Systems, Inc.
Klöckner Hänsel Process Machinery
Knechtel, Inc.
Koco, Inc.
Kraft Food Ingredients

Electric Chocolate Warmer   C.-H. Type

Fruit Drop Rollers and Frame

Adjustab

making, one post-war equipment item did alter the business forever. During the war, candy was produced to be more portable and last longer and the innovations made during WWII subsequently had many looking at how to build a better bar.

Many knew how candy was wrapped, and with what material was key to its marketability. The

s & BRO., Inc.

PHILADELPHIA, PA.

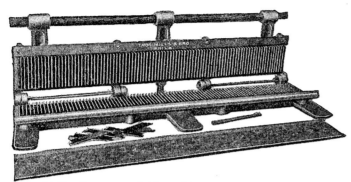

20th Century Adjustable Buttercup Cutter

Pans

Knife Cutters

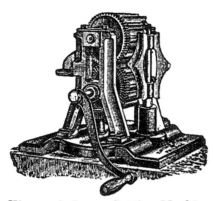

Kiss and Lump Cutting Machine

"Campbell Wrapper" was first developed for the Mars Candy Factory in Chicago, and introduced by Hudson Sharp Co. in the late 1940s. It was soon used throughout the world in the wrapping of candy and perishable goods. The first flow wrappers used glassines and cellophanes. These newfangled machines not only automated wrapping by cutting down on labor, they also

Thomas Mills was established in Philadelphia in 1864. They became one of the leading firms specializing in confectionery equipment. This 1920s catalog sold cutters, copper pans, chocolate moulds, fruit drop rollers, candy jars and scoops.
Catalog Courtesy: Frank Friedwald

P.E. Kramme, Inc.
Latini Enterprises, Inc.
Latini-Hohberger Dhimantec
Leatherhead Food International
Littleford Day Inc.
Loar & Young, Inc.
Lock Inspection Systems
Loders Croklaan
Lodige Process Technology, Inc.
Dr. Paul Lohmann, Inc.
Lonza
MAC Equipment, Inc.
Macintyre Chocolate (LADCO)
P. Magee Enterprises
Mane Inc.
Mantrose-Haueser Co., Inc.
Martek Biosciences Corporation
Massflow Solutions, Inc.
Mastertaste, Inc.
MC/Manufacturing Confectioner
McNeil Nutritionals LLC
Metal Products International, Inc.
Micelli Chocolate Mould Co.
MicroPore Technologies
Miltenberg & Samton, Inc.
Mitsubishi International Food Ingredients
MOD-PAC Corp.
Molded Fiber Glass Tray Co.
Murnane Packaging Corp.
Nealanders International
Nellson Nutraceuticals LLC
Netzsch Fine Particle Technology, LLC.
Nitta Gelatin NA, Inc.
Noveon Hilton Davis Inc.
Nutec Facilities Corp.

Nutrin Corporation
Nutrinova, Inc.
O'Connor & Company, Inc.
O'Hara Technologies, Inc.
O'Laughlin Industries
OPM Chocolate
Orafti Active Food Ingredients
OTT Packagings, Inc.
Ottens Flavors
Palatinit of America Inc.
Palsgaard A/S
Parker Ingredients, LLC
PB Leiner
Penn Quip, Inc.
Petra Foods Limited
Petzholdt-Heidenauer
Pharmachem Laboratories, Inc.
Phoenix Food Ingredients
Pick Heaters, Inc.
Pine Consultants
Pocantico Resources, Inc.
Precision Roll Grinders, Inc.
Printpack, Inc.
JH Process Equipment
Production Techniques Ltd.
Program4 Engineering
Prova, S.A.
Pump & Corrosion Technologies, Inc.
Purac America, Inc.
Qaroma
QC Laboratories
Quadro Engineering
Readco Kurimoto, LLC
Remcon Plastics Inc.
Robertet Flavors

extended the shelf life of products enabling candy makers to distribute to a wider audience.

Many candy companies, in conjunction with their suppliers, created equipment specifically for their brands or unique applications. If useful and innovative, the equipment would soon enter the mainstream of manufacturing and become an industry standard. The Lynch Wrapper, considered the first "fold and tuck" automated wrapper, was first used by Williamson Candy, makers of O Henry! candy bars. Upon realizing its industry worth, Williamson licensed it to the Lynch Machine Company who would go on to sell them to candy bar makers across the country. Henry Heide made a large contribution by developing the first form and fill machine called a "Transwrap." It would become a standard bagging machine for the entire industry.

While candy companies, along with their suppliers, informed and shaped one another, there were also times when innovations and materials were influenced by other businesses. Many early kiss wrap machines were designed to hold a specific width of clear wrapper, much smaller than the size required for other wrapped products. The wrapper size that was used was usually the end of the cellophane roll after it had been cut to accommodate what was needed for another product. These leftover "stump rolls" were a perfect size for candies after they'd been cut down for wrapping cigarette packs.

Cellophane

PACKAGING

Early wholesale confectioners sent their bulk goods to market in paper boxes and wooden crates. Shopkeepers and proprietors in turn would display their treats in glass jars and wooden cases. Consumers would pay for their candy "by the pound" unaware of its origins or ingredient content. Slowly candy companies realized the importance of individually packaging their goods.

By the late 1800s, packaging innovations such as glassine and waxed papers hit the confection market. These products allowed candy makers to individually wrap candy pieces for protection and taste. More importantly, candy makers were able

Whitman's is said to have initiated use of cellophane for candy wrapping in the United States for their Whitman's Sampler. They evidently remained the largest user of imported cellophane from France until around 1924, when DuPont built the first cellophane manufacturing plant in the U.S.
Image Courtesy: Library Of Congress

Romaco, Inc.

Roquette America, Inc.

Charles Ross & Son Company

Rousselot

Rovema Packaging Machines, L.P.

Rudolph Research Analytical

S & S Flavors, Inc.

Safeline, Inc.

Sandvik Process Systems, LLC

Savage Bros. Co.

The Schebler Co.

Wm. A. Schmidt and Sons, Inc.

Schreiber Food Ingredients

The Schwan Food Company

Seltzer Nutritional Technologies

Sensient Colors, Inc.

Sensient Flavors, Inc.

Silesia Flavors

Silliker, Inc.

Silverson Machines, Inc.

Simplex Paper Box Corp.

Smalley Manufacturing Co., Inc.

W. C. Smith Mfg., Inc.

Smiths Detection

Sollich North America, LLC

Specialty Minerals, Inc.

SPI Polyols, Inc.

Spray Dynamics, Ltd.

Springer Pumps, LLC

Star Kay White, Inc.

Stepan Company

Stern Ingredients, Inc.

Strahl & Pitsch, Inc.

Strasburg & Siegel, Inc.

Sweet Packaging

to brand their goods directly on a paper wrapper. Now their candy would last longer due to the barrier and would arrive in edible condition. These once innovative papers have almost entirely given way to plastic and film packaging.

In 1908, Jacques Brandenberger, a Swiss chemist, worked for a French textile factory. While researching methods to make a stain-proof table-cloth, he coated fabric with a thin layer of film. While the tablecloths were not big sellers, his film proved to have enormous potential.

He finally developed a machine that would produce the plastic he coined cellophane. With patents in place he called his company, *La Cellophane*. The name came from combining "cello" from cellulose, with "phane" from the French word diaphane, meaning clear. He began marketing his cellophane in 1919.

In 1927, DuPont created a waterproof lacquer coating that made cellophane especially beneficial to the confection and food industries. The coating meant the plastic was airtight and waterproof. This packaging innovation would pave the way for more plastics and films for various applications to be developed. By the 1940s, cellophane window boxes and polyethylene bags revolutionized the industry. They finally offered confectioners a way to visibly display their attractive product while it stayed fresh and waterproof.

These circa 1920s Minter Bros. matches advertising 7-11 candy bars tout the use of cellophane. Confectioner's usage of the clear wrapping would come to signify fresher product to consumers. Ira Minter, co-founder of the Minter Bros. of Philadelphia was involved in PMCA. Clayton A. Minter served as PMCA president in 1960 and Robert W. Minter in 1964.
Image: Beth Kimmerle Collection

Symrise
Synergy Flavors, Inc.
Tate & Lyle North America
Temuss Products Canada Ltd.
Texture Technologies Corp.
TIC Gums, Inc.
Tinsley Design & Fabricating, Inc.
TMResource, L.L.C.
TNA North America, Inc.
Tomric Systems, Inc.
Tray-Pak Corporation
TRICOR Systems, Inc.
Turbo Systems, Inc.
Ultra Flex Packaging Corp.
Ungerer & Company
Union Confectionery Machinery
Union Process, Inc.
Unique Solutions
Univar USA, Inc.
Varick Enterprises, Inc.
Viking Food Group
Viking Pump
Vink Associates, Inc.
Virginia Dare
WEBBER/SMITH Assoc.
Weber Flavors
WEP Engineering & Consulting
WILD Flavors, Inc.
Wolf Spezialmaschinen GmbH & Co. KG
Alfred L. Wolff, Inc.
Woody Associates, Inc.
WRH Industries, Ltd.
YM Newmark Ltd.

Confectioners Journal

Reg. U. S. Pat. Off.

Established 1874   October, 1928   *Philadelphia, Pa.*

Chapter 6

Confection Industry Organizations and Publications

The confection industry associations listed here are not only PMCA members but also part of our extended family. PMCA would like to acknowledge the collective work they do to help make our confectionery industry thrive.

MEMBERS

American Association of Candy Technologists

(AACT)

The American Cocoa Research Institute

(ACRI)

Chocolate Manufacturers Association

(CMA)

Confectionery Manufacturers of Australasia Ltd.

Confectionery Manufacturers Association of Canada

Korean Chocolate and Cacao Association

(KCCA)

National Confectioners Association

(NCA)

National Confectionery Sales Association

(NCSA)

Penn State University

(PSU)

Retail Confectioners International

(RCI)

World Cocoa Foundation

(WCF)

Established in 1874 by James Parkinson and Edward Heinz, the *Confectioners Journal* is considered the first professional culinary journal published in the United States. Originally a local trade paper, this 1928 nationally distributed edition has advertisements for manufacturers and suppliers alike on the front cover.
Image: Beth Kimmerle Collection

NATIONAL CONFECTIONERS ASSOCIATION

Founded in 1884 in Chicago by representatives of 69 confectionery manufacturing firms, the National Confectioners Association (NCA) is one of the oldest, most respected trade associations in the world.

Over the years, the association has endeavored to provide the kind of vigorous leadership necessary for its members, which include domestic and international confectionery manufacturers and suppliers to the industry to meet the increasingly complex challenges and problems that have confronted the industry.

The National Confectioners Association and its 700 Members congratulate PMCA for reaching its milestone centennial anniversary. It's a true testament to the loyalty and strength of the candy industry that so many of our manufacturers, suppliers and trade associations have been around for a century or more. NCA has enjoyed the relationship it shares with PMCA and we look forward to at least 100 more years of cooperation and collaboration.

—*Larry Graham, NCA*

WORLD COCOA FOUNDATION

The World Cocoa Foundation (WCF) supports cocoa farmers and their families worldwide. WCF programs raise farmer incomes, encourage responsible, sustainable cocoa farming and strengthen communities.

The World Cocoa Foundation (WCF) congratulates PMCA on their 100-year anniversary. This is a significant milestone for a great association!

WCF is a relatively young organization, formed by the chocolate industry in 2000 to support and empower cocoa growing communities in West Africa, Latin America and Southeast Asia. We share many of the same industry members with PMCA.

WCF has always appreciated PMCA's interest in cocoa sustainability, and we have regularly attended each other's meetings to learn from our respective programs and interest areas.

We look forward to the continued collaboration in the future.

—Bill Guyton, World Cocoa Foundation

AMERICAN ASSOCIATION OF CANDY TECHNOLOGISTS

AACT is a premier professional group of individual technologists, operations personnel, educators, students, business staff and others dedicated to the advancement of the confectionery industry.

AACT has its origins at the first PMCA Conference that was held in Bethlehem, Pa. at Lehigh University in 1947. At the time, PMCA was a regional association, based in Pennsylvania USA. During this conference, candy makers, candy technologists and those interested in candy making met to discuss the idea of organizing a national technical association. Hans Dresel, the chairman of the PMCA conference, was also present at this meeting. As part of this meeting they discussed simple problems encountered in candy making such as the boiling and inversion of sugar, why the candy was sticky, dark candy, dull chocolate and everyday problems that still exist even today. Scientifically, they did not know the reason for many problems, what caused them or how to eliminate them. But the candy technologists continued to meet and exchanged ideas on candy making using a more modern approach to benefit candy technologists from all over the country.

The NCA held one of their first meetings with 68 candy manufacturers in attendance, agreeing on membership dues of $10 per year. Shown here is the 7th annual meeting of the National Confectioners Association in 1890, Niagara Falls, N.Y. Image Courtesy: NCA

Back in the early days, candy making was virtually all art and very little science. While it is true that a good candy maker knew what various ingredients did for the candy, very little was understood about why things worked. It was felt that the industry as a whole could benefit from a scientific approach to candy making, pooling the efforts across the industry.

american association of Candy technologists

175 Rock Road, Glen Rock, NJ 07452 USA • Telephone: +1 (201) 652.2655 • Email: aactinfo@gomc.com

NATIONAL COUNCIL

OFFICERS
President
Bob Huzinec
The Hershey Company
First Vice President
Eric Schmoyer
RM Palmer Company
Second Vice President
John Cooke
Cherrydale Farms
Secretary
Patrick Hurley
Spangler Candy Company
Assistant Secretary
Michael Allured
Mfg. / Manufacturing Confectioner
Treasurer
Allen Allured
Mfg. / Manufacturing Confectioner

COUNCILORS AT LARGE
Bill Dyer
Blommer Chocolate Company
Pam Gesford
Perfetti Van Melle USA Inc.
Patrick J. Huffman
The Warrell Corporation
Steve Laning
ADM Cocoa
Jose Sepulveda
Naren Shah
Wm. Wrigley Jr. Company
Scott Yeager
Just Born, Inc.

CHAPTER CHAIRS
California Section
Edward Silva
American Licorice Company
Chicago Section
Michelle Frame
QA Products, Inc.
Milwaukee Section
Richard Hartel
University of Wisconsin, Madison
New Jersey/New York Section
Sonia Hartunian-Sowa
Sharon McGuire
Ardil Foods
Philadelphia Section
Eric Schmoyer
RM Palmer Company

Robert Huzinec
President National Council AACT
c/o The Hershey Company
1025 Reese Avenue
Hershey, PA 17033

April 9, 2007

Ms. Beth Kimmerle
PMCA Centennial Book Editor

The members and council of the AACT would like to congratulate the PMCA on its centennial celebration. The AACT and the PMCA share common roots, as the AACT had its origins at the first PMCA Conference held in Bethlehem, PA at Lehigh University in 1947.

During the past 100 years the PMCA has enhanced the confectionery industry through its courses, seminars, research and academic assistance. These many contributions have allowed the confectionery industry and its members to improve and grow in many ways.

Again congratulations on your centennial and may the next 100 years be even more productive and exciting.

Sincerely,

Bob Huzinec
President, National Council AACT

CHOCOLATE MANUFACTURERS ASSOCIATION

The Chocolate Manufacturers Association (CMA) has served as the premier trade group for manufacturers and distributors of cocoa and chocolate products in the United States since 1923. The association was founded to fund and administer research, promote chocolate to the general public and serve as an advocate of the industry before Congress and government agencies. The American Cocoa Research Institute (ACRI) is the research arm of the Chocolate Manufacturers Association of America. It was founded in 1947 and remains devoted to exploring scientific areas related to cocoa and chocolate.

The Chocolate Manufacturers Association salutes PMCA and its members for 100 years of service, dedication and focus on supporting and advancing the confectionery industry. CMA is honored to share a mission of scientific research and chocolate and cocoa education with PMCA. We look forward to celebrating our industry and all its members at your Gala event in October and for many years to come.

—*Lynn Bragg, President, CMA*

Earl R. Allured consolidated *The Candy Factory* and *The Confectionery Age* magazines and started *The Candy Manufacturer* to cover all aspects of a confectionery manufacturer. With his death in 1931, his wife Prudence would take over and publish the first *Candy Buyers Directory* in 1932. Shown here *The Candy Manufacturer*, June 1921. Image Courtesy: MC Publishing

Vol. 1   **JUNE 1921**   No. 1

The Candy Manufacturer

THE SWEETEST INDUSTRY'S MOST AUTHORITATIVE MAGAZINE

Consolidating

THE CANDY FACTORY

with

THE CONFECTIONERY AGE

An International Magazine of Production and Management for Manufacturing Confectioners

Published by

EARL R. ALLURED

THE CONFECTIONERY BUSINESS PRESS

STOCK EXCHANGE BUILDING
30 NORTH LA SALLE STREET

CHICAGO

$3.00 *the Year*

MANUFACTURING CONFECTIONER

The Manufacturing Confectioner Publishing Company publishes confectionery trade magazines and directories. It was founded in 1921 in Chicago, Ill., and currently has offices in Glen Rock, N.J., and Princeton, Wis. In 2001, the Manufacturing Confectioner celebrated its 80th anniversary as a strong and successful family-owned business. The *Manufacturing Confectioner* is the worldwide business, marketing and technology journal of the candy, chocolate, confectionery, cough drop and sweet baked goods industry. The MC is published once a month and provides in-depth coverage of news, industry statistics, sales and marketing, ingredients, equipment and services.

We at the MC / Manufacturing Confectioner congratulate the PMCA on its first 100 years. The PMCA has grown into the premier technical and production organization for the sweet goods industry with a truly global reach. The MC and the PMCA have had a very close relationship for many years, through the program committee, the research committee and the board of directors. We are proud to have worked with the PMCA on the production of the Proceedings every year including the electronic versions and the Back to

Basics book. PMCA has taken a leadership position in the industry through the annual Production Conference, it's research program, and short courses.

The PMCA Production Conference has grown from its days at Lehigh University, to Franklin & Marshall and now at the Hershey Lodge facilities to the point where it attracts over 900 technical and production personnel from all over the globe. In fact, it is the largest such gathering anywhere in the world.

Congratulations and many happy returns.

—Mike Allured, MC Publishing

CANDY & SNACK BUSINESS

Candy&Snack Business magazine is a trade publication dedicated to the needs of both candy and packaged snack manufacturers. With balanced reporting and the most comprehensive coverage of supplier and industry news, *Candy&Snack Business* provides lively, in-depth strategic and tactical information used to effectively compete in a challenging marketplace.

For its ability to transcend market rivalries by bringing both suppliers and manufacturers together to advance everyone's knowledge and understanding, PMCA can rightly lay claim to ranking among the most highly effective and successful organizations in any industry. Its success in bringing competitors together to forge bonds, both business and personal, is a rare accomplishment that is almost unheard of in any industry. Throughout our association with the organization, PMCA and its members have consistently proven to be remarkable asset for accurate, insightful and useful information for our readers and an educational resource for our staff. As it enters its second century, I'm certain future generations of candy makers will continue to rely on the association as a primary source of accessible information on the practices and challenges that face this remarkable industry and the people who shape it.

—Dave Hoffmann, Editor-in-Chief
Candy&Snack Business

CANDY INDUSTRY MAGAZINE

Candy Industry Magazine is a leading information source for the global confectionery marketplace. *Candy Industry* has chronicled the ever-evolving industry for 63 years and offered readers insight on the latest production efficiencies, innovative packaging, state-of-the-art ingredient technology and marketing trends. *Candy Industry* covers both large and medium-sized confectionery manufacturers, family and privately owned businesses as well as smaller retail confectioners with on-premise manufacturing facilities.

Congratulations to the PMCA on your 100th Anniversary. You've reached far beyond the borders of Pennsylvania over the years and have continued to evolve and respond to the changing needs of the confectionery industry. You are to be congratulated for doing much more than merely existing as an organization for 100 years. Rather you have the distinction of being an organization that is still as relevant in the 21st Century as it was in the early 20th Century.

Stagnito Communications has a number of magazines that have celebrated significant anniversaries, and we appreciate the history we share. We also share your enthusiasm for the future of the confectionery industry and look forward to continuing our relationship for the next 100 years!

—Lisbeth Echeandia, Publisher
Candy Industry Magazine—Stagnito
Communications

JANUARY 1907

CONFECTIONERS JOURNAL

By 1874, the confection business in Pennsylvania was mature enough to warrant the publication of the first trade paper for the candy industry. The *Confectioners Journal*, started by James Parkinson and Edward A. Heintz of Philadelphia, began as a small local paper and soon grew to a substantial resource for confectioners across the United States.

It is considered the first professional culinary journal published in the United States, and according to culinary historian William Weaver, *Confectioners Journal* is "the most important single source for research on American foods in the second half of the nineteenth century." James Parkinson wrote a column for the journal, giving answers to readers' questions on techniques and history. Serving as editor until his death in 1895, he published in its pages recipes from his own collection along with those of other confectioners and bakers. He also included his mother's manuscripts.

His mother was no stranger to the confectionery business. In 1818, Eleanor Parkinson opened a confectionery shop at 180 Chestnut Street in Philadelphia. Her shop was quite successful and soon her husband joined her thriving business. Together they created a celebrated confection establishment with an outstanding reputation, particularly prominent for their hand-made ice creams. In 1843, Eleanor compiled a recipe book, "The Complete Confectioner." Her compilation of sweets and candies is heralded as one of the first comprehensive confection cookbooks in America.

While no longer published, *Confectioners Journal* remains a great resource on the history of the candy industry.

Confectioner Eleanor Parkinson compiled her recipes in her book *The Complete Confectioner*. Considered the first comprehensive collection of confection recipes, it was published and reprinted several times. It was first printed by Philadelphia's publishing house Lea and Blanchard. Shown here is an 1864 edition.
Image Courtesy: Library Of Congress

THE
COMPLETE
CONFECTIONER,
PASTRY-COOK. AND BAKER.

PLAIN AND PRACTICAL

DIRECTIONS FOR MAKING

CONFECTIONARY AND PASTRY,

AND FOR BAKING;

WITH UPWARDS OF FIVE HUNDRED RECEIPTS:

CONSISTING OF

DIRECTIONS FOR MAKING ALL SORTS OF PRESERVES,

SUGAR-BOILING, COMFITS, LOZENGES,

ORNAMENTAL CAKES,

ICES LIQUEURS, WATERS, GUM-PASTE ORNAMENTS
SYRUPS, JELLIES, MARMALADES, COMPOTES,

BREAD-BAKING,

ARTIFICIAL YEASTS, FANCY BISCUITS,

CAKES. ROLLS, MUFFINS, TARTS, PIES, &c. &c.

WITH ADDITIONS AND ALTERATIONS,
BY PARKINSON,
Practical Confectioner, Chestnut Street.

PHILADELPHIA:
J. B. LIPPINCOTT & CO.
1864.

Chapter 7
Our Centennial Year

Many years ago, a small group of Pennsylvania confectioners banded together for solidarity and to regulate the principles of the confectionery industry. One hundred years later, as PMCA celebrates its centennial year, the staff and members of the Centennial Celebration Committee have undertaken writing and producing this anniversary book to mark the history of our organization and to provide a lasting memento of our organization's achievements. It has been an ambitious and exciting undertaking to document the story of an organization dedicated to research, education, and training for the confectionery industry since 1907.

It is our hope that this book will not only be a record of important milestones in PMCA's history but will also provide historical information about member companies and associations who have played an instrumental part in the growth and success of the confectionery industry. The book will be released in conjunction with the PMCA Centennial Gala event in October of 2007.

Our Centennial Celebration Committee also included special publications, tributes and awards at our Centennial Edition Production Conference. Our signature event was held on April 16-18, 2007 in Hershey, Pa. and featured the following unique programs:

2007 Honoree Dinner
Back To Basics Training Book
Hans Dresel Award
Student Outreach Program

A small sampling of the PMCA's honorees attending the 2007 Centennial Production Conference. All honorees received an engraved candy dish as an appreciation of thanks.

2007 HONOREES

Without the continuous efforts and commitment of individuals from PMCA member companies, our association would not have endured and gained the momentum that it has for the past one hundred years.

Dedicated volunteers formed committees which have evolved to arrive at the heart of the Associations mission: to promote the long-term success of the confectionery industry by providing interactive forums for the free exchange of information, to promote and direct basic and applied scientific research, and to educate and train current and future confectionery technical personnel worldwide.

Many volunteers have put forth years of hard work and determination to help bring PMCA to where it stands today. What better way to honor those individuals than during this Centennial Year.

Thank You PMCA Honorees

114

Al Allured

Ronald G. Bixler

Peter Blommer

Larry B. Campbell

Malcolm Campbell

Phil Cartier

Dave Dech

John Glaser

David Goldenberg

Robert Graham

W. David Hess

Patrick Huffman

Peter J. Hughes

Thomas Jackson

Maurice Jeffery

Logan Jones

Martin Krueger

Robert Lukas

Kerwin Martin

Reginald Ohlson

Adrian Timms

Walter Vink

Mary "Dede" Wilson

Thank you for your contributions to the success of PMCA

Past Presidents

Marvin Ames
John Bachman
Peter Blommer
Samuel K. Blumenthal
Clarence G. Bortzfield
Larry B. Campbell
Charles Clark
C.W. Costello
Silvio Crespo
Harry Dangerfield
David Deck
F. Milton Demerath
Arthur Echil
H. Earl Erb
William Fender
Michael Ferraro
Stanley N. Glasbrenner
John Glaser
Otto Glaser
David R. Goldenberg
Carl A. Goldenberg
Harry Goldenberg
Charles Grube

H.C. Heckerman
Peter van B. Heide
Mark Heidelberger
John Henry
John W. Hess
Peter Hughes
Thomas Jackson
William Johnson
Logan Jones
Walter L. Kalbach Jr.
A.C. Keeley
R.F. Keppel
Robert F. Keppel Jr.
C. Rudolph Kroekel
Dr. Douglas Lehrian
R.R. Lloyd
Robert R. Lukas
Joseph A. Marshall Jr.
E.E. McClintock
Daniel McGovern
William Medlicott
E.W. Meyers
Robert W. Minter

Ira Minter
Clayton Minter Jr.
J. Russell Moedinger
A. Rodney Murray
Jay C. Musser
A.J. Napolitan
William A. Newton
Richard M. Palmer Jr.
Richard M. Palmer Sr.
Duane D. Poulterer
William Powers
Achilles Pulakos
William B. Rosskam
Leo Rouf
A.E. Sander
Richard Stark
Charles L. Supplee
David Sykes
Adrian Timms
John Vassos
John Woodward
Philip Wunderle III

HONORARY CONTRIBUTORS

Al Allured
Ronald G. Bixler
Malcolm Campbell
Philip Cartier
Jack Collins
Jayne Collins
Horton Corwin
Dr. Archie Cramer
Hans F. Dresel
William N. Duck
Bob Graham
David Hess
Patrick Huffman
Fred Jacobson
Maurice Jeffery
Marie Kelso
Martin Krueger
Dr. Katheryn Langwill
Kervin Martin
Robert Martin
Alfred Miklos
Donald Mitchell
Reg Ohlson
Fred Paulicka
Carl Pratt
Frank Smullen
Eleanore de Vadetsky
Walter Vink
Rodney Welch
Dede (Young) Wilson

SEVEN YEARS OF BACK TO BASICS

Each year PMCA's Annual Production Conference features a "Back to Basics" training session on a specific topic during the first day of the event. The sessions generally include presentations, video footage, live cooking demonstrations, microscopy and audience sampling, all provided by a highly knowledgeable team of trained professionals in the field. Following the conference, the information from this program is published in the "Annual Production Conference Proceedings," both in print and digital format.

After seven successful Back to Basics productions, the PMCA Production Conference Program committee has prepared a compilation of the training series in the form of a hard copy book. This book is an indispensable reference guide for a variety of industry and collegiate personnel including students of Food Science and related curriculums, those new to the industry as well as those looking to refresh their knowledge or skills on a specific topic.

WCF FARMER PROGRAM

The PMCA's Program committee honored, via the Hans Dresel Memorial Award, the outstanding work done by the World Cocoa Foundation (WCF). To highlight this recognition, PMCA hosted one of the WCF program's outstanding "Master Trainers," who is currently manager of the cocoa sector of a USAID funded project in Northern Ecuador.

World Cocoa Foundation (WCF) programs are helping cocoa farmers, their families and the communities in which they live. These programs are addressing some of the challenges facing cocoa farming families such as crop loss, outdated farming methods and access to markets. Another program affiliated with WCF is Farmer Field Schools (FFS). FFS uses discovery learning and participatory techniques to empower farmers to improve their quality of life using the cocoa tree.

STUDENT OUTREACH PROGRAM

A new Student Outreach Program is under development thanks to a combination of three committees within PMCA. The program began during PMCA's Centennial Year and initial activities took place during the 2007 Annual Production Conference in Hershey, Pa.

The first phase of the program allowed for a select number of students, from educational institutions with top Food Science and related programs, to attend the conference. The students were recognized during the Monday evening dinner, received a copy of the "Back to Basics" training series book, (2000-2006), and had the opportunity to network with a variety of company personnel to gain knowledge of the industry and investigate career opportunities.

Alfredo Duenas Davalos (left), FFS Master Trainer and industry consultant from Ecuador, and B.K.Matlick (right), represented the World Cocoa Foundation at PMCA's 2007 Centennial Production Conference.

Left to Right: Lihe Yeo, Bridget Schigoda, Heather Mendenhall, Renee Lietha, Pawel Domejczyk, Carol Dicolla, and Adrian Timms, PMCA President. The science students were recognized at PMCA's 2007 Centennial Production Conference.

PMCA ADMINISTRATIVE ACKNOWLEDGEMENT

Our past and present PMCA administrative staff has been immensely loyal. We recognize them here for each of the 61 production conferences they have pulled off and for the cheer and efficiency they have brought to their everyday duties. Each has brought to PMCA not only their individual skills but dedication and pride in her work and our confection business.

- **Marie Kelso 1949-1987**

- **Jayne Collins 1987-1992**

- **Dede (Young) Wilson 1992-2004**

- **Yvette Thomas 2003-**

A few notes from and about our PMCA Administration:

Marie Kelso

SERVED PMCA 1949-1987

Marie Kelso served as Secretary to the Production Conference Committee for 38 years, and indeed her name became synonymous with the event itself. In her youth she was secretary to Hans Dresel, a salesman for Felton Chemical Company located in Philadelphia, Pa. As her boss worked tirelessly to organize and promote PMCA's Annual Production Conference, as well as AACT events, she prepared and managed diligently as well. After she left her job at Felton Chemical, the Production Conference became her life's work. Marie was also active for many years in the Philadelphia Section of AACT. Marie Kelso passed away in September 1995.

The PMCA's Board of Directors established an award in Marie's honor in 1997. It is given each year to the author of the paper presented at the previous year's Annual Production Conference that most significantly contributes to industry knowledge.

Jayne Collins

SERVED PMCA 1987-1992

Kudos to all who have contributed to the PMCA during the past 100 years, many blazing **New Trails** and making a big **Skor** in furthering PMCA's goals.

My years with PMCA started in 1987 with the preparation for the '88 Production Conference and locating a new home for the Conference. With the help of many, particularly (**The 3 Musketeers**) the late John Hess, El Myers and Dr. Rodney Welsh, the most viable location was selected—The Hershey Lodge & Convention Center.

The first Conference to be held at The Hershey Lodge & Convention Center was in 1988, with 714 in attendance, representing an increase of 33 percent over the prior year, and the speakers all **Stars** with no **Airheads** or **Milk Duds** identified.

The following years, during my period with PMCA, saw periods of an **Overload** of work and I cannot say that **Zero** mistakes were made, but none appeared to be **Whoppers**. The Conference attendance continued to increase and we were fortunate to obtain many great speakers, mostly **Smarties** and hearsay has it that none were **Dum Dums**. Never did one hear **Snickers**, but rather, many a time one could hear the **Krackel** of excitement.

It was indeed a pleasure and an honor to serve PMCA, a **Sweet Indulgence** with **Mounds** of great memories of wonderful people and times—**Treasures** to be remembered.

—Jayne Collins
Theme inspired by a letter received
from John Hess in 1988

Dede (Young) Wilson

SERVED PMCA 1992-2004

During my tenure with PMCA I witnessed the transformation of the association into a vibrant, forward-moving organization, internationally recognized for the integrity of their programs and the benchmark for excellence in confectionery science and technology. Looking back, the key to that transformation was the Strategic Planning retreat in the early 1990s. We sensed we were poised at a crossroads. Who were we? What did we want the association to look like in 2007? Even then, we recognized the significance of the Centennial year. The result was the formulation of the Vision and Mission Statements. During the years that followed, the leadership drew on them to chart the best way forward, to stay focused on their defined mission, and to preserve their unique and valuable heritage.

At that time the path in front of us needed careful preparation, since moving forward obligated the association to step out of the comfortable niche of its Pennsylvania roots. Over the years we gradually implemented a new corporate color palate, a new name, new logo, new financial organization, a complete Research mission reorganization, expansion of short courses, a web page, and a cutting edge series in the conference Back to Basics program. The final step was a thorough and well-conceived revision of the bylaws that opened seats on the Board of Directors to non-Pennsylvania companies, while preserving some seats to honor and preserve the heritage. We had struck that elusive balance!

Although my time with PMCA is over, the warm bond remains since I still refer to 'we' when I speak of PMCA. I derived enormous job satisfaction as Administrative Director because I sensed I was working with a very unique group, one that was exceptionally steadfast and unwavering in its dedication to their Vision and Mission.

—Dede (Young) Wilson

Yvette Thomas

PMCA SERVICE BEGAN
2003

I joined PMCA on March 1, 2003, and had the honor of opening and staffing the first permanent office in July of that year. The creation of a permanent office and regrouping its records and small library, at a single location, was a big undertaking and helped to provide a solid framework for permanence and growth. The PMCA staff is looking forward to supporting the members, officers, directors and committees in their mission to bring world-class research, education, and training to the global confectionery industry. I am confident that the unique foundation PMCA has created in the last 100 years of friendship and cooperation will serve it well in supporting its membership as it rises to the challenges and opportunities of a world economy increasingly focused on diversity and quality.

—Yvette Thomas

"Three Friends" depicts an animated, young girl smitten with her Hershey product and is an early example of Hershey's turn-of-the-century promotional advertising art. It was used as an in-store poster around 1900 when Hershey was still making cocoa and milk chocolate in Lancaster, Pa.
Image Courtesy: The Hershey Archives

Index

BEST SELLING PENNY CANDIES

Suckers

2 for 1c Suckers
YO-350—300 in box.

Box **$1.12**

"Razzbo"—Largest 2 for 1c size on market, 5 flavors and colors, guaranteed in all climates.

YO-351—4 boxes in carton.

Carton **$2.95**

4 Kinds Asstd.—Largest sizes, wrapped. 120 in box, asstd. 1 box each. World Suckers, Radio Suckers, Caramel Suckers and Big League.

Y-732—120 in box.
Box **72c**

Butter Scotch Sweet Roll— 6 in. long, wax paper wrapped.

Y-1342—120 in box.
Box **72c**

Ping Pong—Pure sugar suckers, asstd. color combinations, designs and flavors.

Y-1897—100 in box.
Box **72c**

"Big Hit"—Extra large fluffy center, asstd. flavors with chocolate coating.

Y-1344—120 in box.
Box **72c**

Big League—Extra large, asstd. flavors and colors, decorated wax paper wrapped.

Y-1191—120 in box.
Box **72c**

Charm Pops—True fruit flavors, orange, cherry, raspberry, grape, etc., wrapped.

Y-1060—120 in box.
Box **72c**

Reed's "Butter Pal"—Butterscotch, each wrapped.

PEPPERMINT CREAM BAR

Y-324—72 pcs. in box.

Box **52c**

Peppermint Cream Bar—¾ oz., peppermint cream center, chocolate coated, foil wrapped.

COCOANUT CREAM BAR

Y-323—72 pcs. in box.

Box **52c**

Cocoanut Cream Bar—¾ oz., cocoanut cream center, chocolate coated, foil wrapped.

CHOCOLATE "GOLD COINS"

Sell 5 for 5c or 1c each

Y-1212—456 in chest in box..........Box **$3.20**
"Chest O' Gold"—1½ in. pure chocolate "coins" covered with gilt foil, extra heavy iron chest, gilt bronze decorated. Chest will sell for 75c.

FOIL WRAPPED CHOCOLATE KISSES

Y-1242 — 290 pcs. (2½ lbs.) in box.   Box **55c**

Sweet milk chocolate, foil wrapped.

"CHICKEN DINNER" 1c BARS

Y-1134—100 in box

Box **75c**

Jumbo size, maple cream center, caramel and peanuts, milk chocolate coated, wrapped.

"WILBUR" NUT LUNCH BARS

Suggested 10 for 10c Retailer
Y-1769—240 in carton.

Carton **$1.85**

¾ oz., sweet milk chocolate, filled with roasted peanuts, double wrapped.

TOOTSIE ROLLS

Y-1903—120 in box.
Box **69c**

Chocolate chewing center, wrapped.

LICORICE CANDIES

Y-1218—120 in box.
Box **72c**

Long Cable Twist—Sweet licorice.

RAINBOW "BABY WAFERS"

Y-1210—100 rolls in carton.   Carton **69c**

23 sugar wafers in roll, asstd. colors and flavors. Largest penny roll on the market!

RAINBOW "SWEETIES"

Y-1211—100 tubes in carton.   Carton **67c**

2¾ in. tube, filled with candy pellets, asstd. colors and flavors, transparent face opening.

"BABY RUTH" MINTS

Y-343—Chocolate
Y-344—Mint
Y-345—Wintergreen
Y-346—Orange Box **72c**
100 rolls in box

"BABY RUTH" FRUIT DROPS

Y-327—Lemon
Y-328—Lime
Y-329—Orange Box **75c**
100 rolls in box.

Pure sugar candies, triple wrapped, heat sealed, 10 tablets in roll.

"CURTISS" 1c BARS

Y-332—100 in box
Box **75c**

"Baby Ruth"—Over ¾ oz., caramel roll, chocolate coated, wrapped.

Y-337—100 in box.
Box **75c**

"Ostrich Egg"—Soft pure white marshmallow center, chocolate coated, wrapped.

Y-330—100 in box.
Box **75c**

"Butter Finger"—Over ¾ oz., peanut butter stick, chocolate coated, wrapped.

Y-334—100 in box
Box **75c**

"Buy Jiminy"—Over ¾ oz., peanut bar, wrapped

Y-335—100 in box
Box **75c**

"Milk Nut Loaf"—Soft creamy marshmallow center, roasted nut meat topping, allover coated with heavy milk chocolate.

Y-336—100 in box.
Box **75c**

"I Scream Bar"—Over ¾ oz., cream layer wafer, chocolate coated, wrapped.

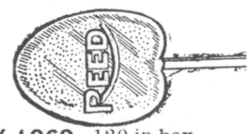